Czech Immigrants and the Sokol Movement

*To Clara Olesonova
and a long friendship
Bob*

Robert M Tomanek

Robert J. Tomanek

Penfield
BOOKS™

Acknowledgments

The author appreciates those individuals who assisted, in various ways, with the preparation of this book. These include Martin Nekola, Norma Zabka, Ed Chlanda, Rome Milan, Ellen Garlicki Nyemcsik, Jean Dusek and Joan Sedlacek. A special thanks to David Muhlena, librarian of the National Czech and Slovak Museum and Library, for his help in locating and sharing resources, and to Zora Machková of the Czech National Archives, and Kateřina Pohlová and Marcela Janouchová of the Czech Sokol organization, who provided valuable historical information and photographs. The book cover was created by Rita Tomanek, as were the sketches in the text. Paul Reimann was responsible for technical support regarding photographs and graphics. The financial support of Czech Foreign Affairs Ministry helped with the cost of the book's preparation and publication. Finally, the author is grateful to his Czech immigrant parents for teaching him their language and culture.

About the Cover

The watercolor painting on the cover, by Rita Tomanek, suggests that the Statue of Liberty is coming through the mist and ocean to meet the Czech family as they are arriving in America. A gymnast with a Sokol flag represents their gift of culture to their new homeland.

Editing by: Deb Schense and Melinda Bradnan.

Cover art design by: Rita Tomanek
Cover layout by: Deb Schense
Printed in the U.S.A.

Penfield Books
215 Brown Street
Iowa City, IA 52245
1-800-728-9998
www.penfieldbooks.com

About the Author

Photo by Joan Liffring-Zug Bourret

Robert J. Tomanek

Robert J. Tomanek, Ph.D. is Professor Emeritus of Anatomy and Cell Biology at the University of Iowa, Iowa City, Iowa, where he specialized in cardiovascular science. He is a first generation American, born in Omaha in 1937, to Czech immigrant parents. His parents were active in the Omaha Czech community and insisted that their sons were able to speak Czech and partake in the culture of their native land.

Robert met his wife, Rita, a native of Cedar Rapids, through Sokol. Her parents were both descendants of Czech immigrants. The Tomaneks travel regularly to the Czech Republic to visit relatives, and in 2015, Robert authored the book: *Moravia: Gem of the Czech Republic.*

Subsequently, as a board member of the Sokol Museum and Library, he recognized the need to help preserve the history of the Sokol movement, which is an important component of the Czech immigrant history.

Contents

"Perhaps our brightest hope for the future lies in the lessons of the past. The people who have come to this country have made America in the words of one perceptive writer, 'a heterogeneous race but a homogeneous nation.'"

—John F. Kennedy: *A Nation of Immigrants,* 1953.

Introduction

In February 1862, Dr. Miroslav Tyrš and Jindřich Fügner formed Prague Sokol, a gymnastic club dedicated to the "pursuit of physical training." They believed that a well-structured gymnastics program was the basis of the physical and moral health of individuals and the nation. The philosopher Tyrš was a visionary who believed that a Sokol "movement" would motivate and inspire the Czech people and revive a personal and national consciousness, at a time when Bohemia and Moravia were under the Habsburg's Austrian rule. Tyrš' was a Renaissance man whose vision of the Sokol movement went beyond physical training to include the concepts of democracy, equality, brotherhood, liberty, and civic responsibility. His Sokol movement was based on his understanding of the principles of national life. First, gymnastic training was intended for both the physical and moral health of the nation, for all classes, young and old, male and female. Second, he viewed gymnastics as an expression of the artistic instinct of man that is of equal importance with the fine arts.

More than a century and a half later, we can see that the Sokol movement played a significant role in history. It was a major force in forming the Czech people's drive for independence and the formation of Czechoslovakia in 1918. This birth of a new nation occurred by transforming Czech nationalism into a movement of the masses, especially by its role in the formation of the Legion, the army of men who joined the allies and fought against Austria and its allies. Moreover, Sokol clubs in the United States served as ethnic centers for families by providing fitness through gymnastics as well as Czech culture, e.g., libraries, theatre, dance, and music. Sokol and the German Turnverein were the main organizations that introduced Americans to gymnastics. The Sokol movement is an integral part of the of the history of Czech settlers in America, and is a testimony regarding the influence of one man's vision for an ethnic heritage. The wide-ranging effects of the Sokol movement can hardly be over-emphasized. Sokol and Czech patriotism were closely related and together they inspired self-confidence in the Czech people. During World War II, Sokol members were a major force in the resistance to Nazi occupation of Bohemia and Moravia, and many were imprisoned or executed for their patriotism.

This book focuses on Czech settlers in America, their cultural contributions, and the role of the Sokol movement that was a powerful force in the Czech-American communities. Czech immigrants and their successive generations lived in their own communities, had their own churches, and national homes (Čapek, 1926, 9). They formed their own national organizations and had their own ideologies. Without abandoning their values and culture, they assimilated into the American way of life. The Czech immigrant story is one of a quest for freedom and opportunity in a new land and the role of their culture, which enabled their success. The Sokol movement was a unifying component of their Czech culture.

The first part of this book addresses the climate in which the Sokol movement was born and how the movement influenced the Czech people's quest for nationhood and ethnic identity. Consideration is given to the struggles of the Sokol clubs, both internal and under the rule of the Habsburg Austrian Empire and subsequently the Austro-Hungarian Dual Monarchy (Chapter 1). The period spanning the years between the two world wars was characterized by an impressive growth of Sokol clubs and their contributions to gymnastics, physical education, and fitness programs. It was during this period that the Sokol movement in the first Czechoslovak Republic flourished, and is the topic of Chapter 2.

Chapter 3 details the Czech immigrant's settlements in the US, their culture, and the role of Sokol in their communities. These Czech settlers, like other ethnic groups, made significant contributions to American life. However, Czechs had the advantage of a high literacy rate (97%); moreover many were tradesmen, and some were professionals. These characteristics aided them in their community life. In Chapter 4 attention is given to individual Sokol clubs. They played important roles in their communities and contributed to gymnastics, fitness, and Czech-American culture. The determination of the Czech settlers to establish and maintain Sokol clubs is a tribute to their willingness to sacrifice for the good of family life and culture. Sokols in the US made major contributions to the sport of gymnastics by developing outstanding gymnasts, coaches, judges, and other officials (Chapter 5). These very significant contributions have often been overlooked in the Sokol literature. Finally, in Chapter 6 the factors that have contributed to the decline of Sokols in the US are discussed, as well as those that have facilitated the survival and success of various Sokol clubs.

Definition of some words and terms in this book

Organizations

ASO: American Sokol Organization established in 1917.

ČSPS: Česko-Slovanský Podporující Spolek (Czech-Slovak Protective Society): a forerunner of ZCBJ, a fraternal group that worked with Sokol clubs and often shared facilities with them.

ČOS: Česká Obec Sokolská (Czech Organization Sokol)

NUS: Národní Jednota Sokolská (National Unity Sokol), the first Czech-American national Sokol organization (founded in 1879 and was replaced by American Sokol Organization in 1917).

Slovanská Lípa (Slavic Linden): A literary society that was sometimes united with Sokol clubs, e.g., T.J. Sokol in Chicago founded in 1866, merged with Slavic Linden in 1866.

Sokol USA: A Slovak gymnastic organization founded as Slovak Gymnastic Unit Sokol in 1896 and became Sokol USA in 1962.

ZCBJ: (Západní Česko-Bratrská Jednota (Western Bohemian Fraternal Association), an organization that sometimes-shared facilities with Sokol clubs and aided them financially.

Geography and Ethnicity

Bohemia: The western part of the Czech Republic, that includes Prague, the capital.

Czech lands: The lands that were ruled by Bohemian kings, i.e., Bohemia, Moravia, Czech Silesia.

Czechs: Citizens of the Czech Republic; historically, the term included only Bohemians.

Moravia: The eastern part of the Czech Republic, that includes Brno, its main city.

Ruthenia: This small country, located between Russia and Hungary became part of Czechoslovakia in 1919, but was ceded to the Soviet Union in 1945.

Silesia: One of the three parts of the traditional Czech lands, along with Bohemia and Moravia. It is now the northeastern part of Moravia.

Slavic nations: 1) East—Belarus, Russia and Ukraine; 2) West—Czech Republic, Poland and Slovakia; 3) South—Bosnia and Herzegovina, Bulgaria, Croatia, Macedonia, Montenegro, Serbia and Slovenia

Other

Slet: Rally or Gathering, a celebration every four or five years that included exhibitions of mass calisthenics, competitions in gymnastics and other sports, parades and numerous cultural events.

Nazdar: Sokol greeting meaning "to success."

Tužme se: A call to Sokol members meaning "let us harden ourselves."

Note: Reference citations in the text are given by author's name, year of publication and page or pages cited.

1

The Sokol Movement: A Czech Vision

Birth of the Movement

The Czech Lands

Centuries of self-rule. For eighty years, during the 9th century, Bohemians and Moravians were citizens of the Great Moravian Empire, which included what later became Czechoslovakia; this empire also included parts of Poland and Austria. Great Moravia was established by the unification of various Slavic tribes. The heirs of most of this empire were Bohemian princes and the clan of Přemyslids; they ruled the "Czech lands" which included Bohemia, Moravia, and a part of Silesia. While Bohemian is synonymous with Czech, "Czechs" denotes Moravians and Bohemians who share a common language (Laska, 1978, vii). From 1306–1525 Bohemia and Moravia were ruled by the Luxembourgs. King Karel (Charles) IV ruled during the "Golden Age" of Medieval Bohemia, and is remembered for founding important cultural institutions, especially Prague University (later called Charles University), developing domestic intellectuals, promoting the arts, and erecting many buildings (Agnew, 1992, 32–36). During his reign, Bohemia became both powerful and wealthy.

Loss of autonomy. In 1526, Ferdinand I, a member of the Habsburg family, became King of Bohemia and consolidated royal power, thereby curbing the autonomy of Prague and other cities. The Czechs lost their traditional right to elect a king. "Thereafter, the Czech lands were gradually, but inexorably, incorporated into what eventually became the Austrian Empire" (Sager, 1998, 42). Adding fuel to the fire, a century later, Ferdinand II executed twenty-seven Czech aristocrats and, for many years after, publicly displayed their heads. Czechs were subjected to Habsburgs-Austrian rule until 1867, and then by the Habsburgs when they merged with the Hungarian Empire to form a dual monarchy (Austro-Hungarian Empire). This subjugation lasted until the end of World War I, when the Czechs and Slovaks were united in the First Czechoslovak Republic, a union that lasted until the country was divided by Germany in 1939; Bohemia and Moravia were occupied by the Germans and considered a Protectorate of Germany. In contrast, Slovakia declared itself a new state, but never the less became a puppet of Germany. Thus, the Habsburg's ruled the Czech lands from 1526 to 1918. The map in Figure 1 (following page) illustrates the geography of the Austrian and Hungarian Empires in 1918.

The Czech identity and determination. This historical background is relevant for the understanding of the Czech identity and culture, and especially the Czech mindset and circumstances during the 19th century. Czechs enjoyed self-rule from the ninth century through the early 16th century, and then lost their independence, and saw their Czech language subjugated to that of German. This historical change had a profound effect on the Czech identity. The effects of these losses on the eventual determination and mindset of the Czech people cannot be overstated. One can then begin to understand and appreciate the climate in which the Sokol movement began, and how it contributed significantly to the formation of Czechoslovakia in 1918.

The Austrian Empire and Habsburg Rule

Nineteenth century European conditions. The Habsburg dynasty supported the Catholic faith, a factor that caused many Czechs to recall the Hussite movement that was a response to the killing of Jan Hus, a preacher who sought reforms in the Catholic Church. Some of his radical followers fought the Crusaders, and brought about religious dualism for a period of time. However, the Catholic Habsburgs were not supportive of non-Catholic faiths, which in turn fostered Czechs to resent both the Habsburgs and Catholicism. This history played a role in Czech attitudes and became the source of anti-clericalism, which found its way into the Sokol movement. One must appreciate that 19th century Europe was characterized

POLAND

SILESIA

GALICIA

UKRAINE

★ Praque

CZECH REPUBLIC   Moravia

Bohemia

SLOVAKIA

★ Brno

GERMANY

Bratislava

Vienna ★

★ Budapest

AUSTRIA

HUNGARY

ROMANIA

SLOVENIA

CROATIA

★ Zagreb

ITALY

SERBIA

BOSNIA
HERZEGOVINA

Figure 1. What is now the Czech Republic was part of the Austrian Empire (indicated by the dotted background) when the Sokol movement began in 1862. Slovakia was under Hungarian rule (dashes indicate Hungarian Empire).

by monarchical forms of government, a fact that people endured, and considered too difficult to overthrow. Nevertheless, the discontent among the Czech people ran deep.

Czech concerns for an identity grow. The social hierarchy of Bohemia in the 18th century was dominated by aristocrats, who tended to be non-national. However, by the mid-19th century, the intellectual elite began articulating a sense of community and identifying with Czech nationhood. This caused a greater awareness that the nation's identity is based on ethnicity and, especially, language. In 1848, revolutions, which began in Sicily, spread across Europe, but the Austrian Empire withstood the storm. In order to avoid prison or execution, the Czechs who participated in the revolution were forced to flee their country (Stavařová, 2009, 27). Although the ruling Habsburgs made some concessions to various groups (including the establishment of civic clubs and festivals), the legal, national, and cultural identification of the Czechs was not realized, and they remained under Austrian absolutism until the end of World War I. Before the 1848 revolutions, Karel Havlíček Borovský (1821–1856), a journalist-publisher and liberal nationalist was a strong voice for freedom. He is considered the father of Czech journalism. By drafting a program of a modern Czech democracy, and publishing his writings in his national newspaper, he reached and awakened the Czech people.

It was the support of some of the elite citizens that encouraged the middle-class and peasants to become more nationalistic; this awakening sparked an ethnic identity and led to a Czech cultural revival during the mid-19th century. As described by Panek and Tůma (2009, 331): "The neo-absolute regime's gradual thawing, following the Austrian army's defeat in the war with Sardinia and France in 1859, was an impulse for reviving the political activities of the people living under the Habsburg monarchy." One such activity was the formation of the liberal National Party. František Rieger, the son-in-law of František Palacký (one of the three fathers of the Czech nation) was at the center of the nationalist movement. By 1861, the *Nařodní Listy* National Paper was established by Julius Grégr. One Czech concern was that the ruling Habsburgs were "Germanizing" the Czech culture, most notably by the fact that their native language was secondary to German, the official language.

Equality of Czechs with Austrians. The historian František Palacký wrote a chronicle of the Czech people and called for a separate, but equal nation within Austria, which embraced the creed of the Czech national movement as "Austro-Slavism." He hoped that this identity would create a buffer against both German and Russian expansionism. There was already a movement for a revival by Czechs, fostered by small groups of intellectuals, and a cultural revival under the patronage of aristocratic families who sponsored scholars, and founded museums and societies. Slovaks, under Hungarian rule, were also beginning to look forward to their independence. Despite these considerations by small groups, German and Hungarian liberals were fervent for their own nationalism and did not support the Czech and Slovak national movements. In the mid-1800s, Josef Dobrovský, a linguist, codified Czech, and Josef Jungmann compiled the first Czech dictionary. Then nationalists at Prague University (later named Charles University) won an important victory when a separate Czech-speaking faculty was added. Czechs constituted about one-fifth of the eleven ethnic groups living in the Austro-Hungarian Empire. They made many significant cultural contributions, including establishing the National Theater and the National Museum in Prague in 1883 and 1890, respectively. The national revival also was aided by the annual Czech Ball *(Národní Beseda)* where only Czech was spoken.

Czech emancipation. As noted by Panek and Tůma (2009, 295–6), Czechs in the late 18th and 19th centuries, were "a non-ruling nation or ethnic group, which did not equal a state community." Rather than a single revolution, Czech emancipation evolved in stages. Initially there was a scientific interest in their ethnicity (1780–1810), followed by two decades of national agitation, sparked by some who wanted a single nation for Czechs. Finally, following the 1848 revolutions staged against monarchies, most Czechs favored the idea of membership in a nation with specific values.

Tomáš Masaryk's early role in an independent Czech state. As the 20th century neared, discussions among the intellectuals intensified, and in 1896 the Czechoslovak Union was formed through the efforts of Masaryk (1850–1937), his Czech compatriot Edvard Beneš (1884–1948) and Milan Rastislav Štefánik (1880–1919), a Slovak astronomer and general in the

French army. This organization served as the prelude to the establishment of Czechoslovakia twenty-two years later. Masaryk, a Full Professor, supported Slovak students who advocated cooperation with the Czechs for their national identities. In 1914, World War I was triggered by the assassination of Archduke Franz Ferdinand and his wife in Sarajevo, Bosnia by a Serbian nationalist, who was part of a liberation coup struggling to end Austro-Hungarian rule of Bosnia and Herzegovina. Austria and Hungary blamed the Serbian government for the attack and declared war on Serbia (a Slavic nation) and gained the support of Germany, the Ottoman Empire and Bulgaria. Serbia was joined by France, Great Britain, and Russia. The Russian revolution in 1917 brought a halt to their participation on the side of the allies. However, the US entered the war in support of France and Great Britain in 1917.

Masaryk, a Sokol member who exercised daily, continued his advocacy for a Czechoslovak nation during the war years and traveled to Great Britain and the US. He envisioned Sokol as a force in developing a Czech ethnic core. His activities in America were notably successful and culminated in Philadelphia's Constitution Hall of Independence. It was in the "city of brotherly love" that the Czech people's long dream of independence became a reality when the allies recognized the Czechoslovak National Council as the first government of the new nation, with T.G. Masaryk as its first president. This accomplishment was aided by President Woodrow Wilson, who to this day is honored by Czechs and Slovaks.

Masaryk and the Czechoslovak legionnaries. At the onset of World War I, some Czech and Slovak soldiers, not wanting to fight the allies, united with the Russian army to fight against Austrians and Germans. They were joined by some of their comrades from Russian prisoner of war camps. By 1917 this group (of which about 8% of its members were Slovaks) had grown substantially, and from this group Tomas Masaryk helped form a band of fighters called the Czechoslovak Legion. When the Bolsheviks came into power, they signed peace terms with Germany, which left the legionnaires the task of fighting the Germans alone in Russia. When the Bolsheviks ordered the legionnaries to disarm, they overthrew the local Bolsheviks and went on to sweep aside their forces along the entire length of the Trans-Siberian Railway. After the

two groups signed an armistice with the 5th Red Army, they were allowed safe passage to the very distant town of Vladivostok, a journey that took two years. At its peak, the Czechoslovak Legion consisted of about 60,000 legionnaries. The story of this group of brave men is a testimony to the determination of Bohemian, Moravian, and Slovak people's quest for independence and has been documented in a book by McNamara (2016).

The Philosopher Miroslav Tyrš (1832–1884) and the Sokol Idea

Early life. Tyrš, born Friedrich Emanuel Tirsch in Northern Bohemia in 1832, moved with his German speaking family to Vienna. Friedrich was orphaned at age six, and was adopted by his uncle in Bohemia after his parents and two younger sisters all died of tuberculosis. Later a second uncle adopted him, and young Friedrich moved to Prague to live with him and his family. There he grew up in contact with Czech peasants, an experience that awakened his "Czech consciousness." At the age of twelve he enrolled in therapeutic gymnastics. Four years later Fredrich participated in the Slavic Congress in Prague, an event that strengthened his "conviction of a fully conscious Bohemian and Slav being" (Bábela & Oborný, 2018, 314). While studying philosophy at Prague University, Tyrš, which later became his adopted name, began to identify with Czechs and their goals of freedom and national identity. He participated in gymnastic training at Malýpetrův Institute and then at Schmidt's Gymnastic Institute; both clubs used Friedrich Ludwig Jahn's Turnverein system. Therefore, Tyrš knew the details and philosophy of the German gymnastic system. Subsequently, he worked as a trainer in a therapeutic gymnastic institute under Ferdinand Schmidt, while he was studying for his Ph.D., which he competed in 1860.

Tyrš, the Renaissance man. Dr. Miroslav Tyrš came forth with penetrating insight and recognized that the time for a national rebirth had arrived. He was a scholar, art critic, and parliamentary delegate, who studied classical Greece. He was impressed by its civic virtues and physical training that underscored the Greek culture and national unity. Tyrš understood that these Greek characteristics inspired this ethnic group to establish the Olympic Games. He reasoned that national survival, especially for a small nation, depended on the development of man's nature: a truthful, good, and beautiful soul housed in a strong and healthy body. Freedom, he concluded, was humanity's most precious possession. His vision, enhanced by his own training and teaching of gymnastics, emphasized that physical training should be systematic and regular, and based on discipline (national, civic, and personal). Moreover, his goal for the Sokol movement was to include all classes of society, all political parties, religions, and both sexes. These aims supported the eventual establishment of a Czech democratic nation and were embraced by Czech patriots. Tyrš' credibility was enhanced by his prestige as a scholar and his philosophy of inclusion of Czechs from all walks of life.

Inspiration for the Sokol movement. Karel Havlíček Borovský, a journalist, who with the historian, Palacký, led the National Liberal Movement and was the first editor of a Czech political journal in which he addressed Czech grievances (Jandásek, 1932). Havlíček fought for a political foundation guarantee by the constitution and the emperor by defending free speech and seeking an end to censorship and repression. Considered a radical by the government, he was exiled to Tyrol in Italy and died upon his return to his homeland. He was viewed as a martyr and revered for his selfless fight for the Czech's struggle for nationhood. It was six years after Havlíček Borovský's death that Tyrš began his quest for a Sokol movement, which reflected the values of this heroic journalist. The great Sokol project (Jandásek, 1932), as envisioned by Tyrš, was aimed at creating:

> ...a new race, stouter than its predecessors, which, in a strong body preserving a strong will, would once more unite with the dovelike meekness of the Slav, the falcon-like boldness of more glorious times; a race which would recognize rights of others, while holding fast to its own, and in days of tempest and storm would weld itself as of old into an impregnable barrier, on which all attacks of our enemies would be shattered.

Tyrš, the scholar and Czech National. As an academic, Tyrš' involvement with Czech nationals led him to change his first name from Friedrich to the Czech name, Miroslav. Following his doctoral studies, Tyrš contributed to a Czech encyclopedia, during which time he worked with František Rieger, who was a son-in-law of František Palacký, a historian who supported an Austro-Slavic Federal Austria composed of nationalities with equal rights. Rieger's work brought him into the circle of intellectuals who were working toward the goal of renewing the Czech culture. The German Turnverein was already in existence for five decades, having been established in 1811 by Friedrich Ludwig Jahn. Tyrš was impressed by Jahn's philosophy of love for the fatherland through gymnastics and his inclusion of both romanticism and progressive values. Memberships were opened to all classes. Tyrš envisioned a similar movement in the Czech lands, but one that would be adapted to a Czech national consciousness.

Tyrš the gymnast. It is important to remember that Tyrš was a gymnast and was involved with two prominent Prague clubs (Schmidt's and Malýpetr's), thus, his Sokol vision was grounded in physical training, as a foundation of, not an addition to, a philosophy. In 1861, some gymnasts from Schmidt's Institute invited Tyrš to join a group interested in forming a gymnastics club. However, the club took the name "Prague Turnverein." Consequently, Tyrš enlisted the support of a promising Czech gymnast, Jan Malýpetr, who was able to provide space for a gymnasium. As detailed in *Památník Sokola Pražského* (1883, 49–52), the gym was well-equipped with outdoor space provided for summer training. Malýpetr was also an asset, because he had earned a university degree in the teaching of gymnastics, and he made the facility available as soon as Prague Gymnastic Association was established. Also, some people of influence, including Julius Grégor, editor of *Národny Listy,* an important Czech newspaper, and his brother Edvard joined the cause (Garver, 1977, 77). They supported the idea of a Czech Gymnastic Club in Prague, with its purpose being the "pursuit of physical training."

The first Sokol club. In 1862, the Prague Gymnastic Club became Sokol Prague under the banner of a falcon (Sokol is the Czech word for falcon), and the Sokol constitution was approved enabling the foundation for the Sokol movement. The new organization grew "like an avalanche," because men joined without urging *(Památník Sokola Pražského* 1883, 49–52). They could train several days per week in a well-equipped gym, and were able to be members of a fully Czech ethnic club. Josef Mánes designed the Sokol

Club flag, made of red and white silk with *"Tužme se"* (let us harden ourselves) on one side, and "Sokol" on the other. Over the first seven years of the club's existence, its membership grew to 807 men. As soon as Prague Sokol was formed, it became a concern for the authorities, who feared that the club could include radical politicians. For this reason, police sat in on meetings held by the club, as early as the first six months of its formation.

Tyrš and Fügner Collaborate to Establish Sokol

Jindřich Fügner (1822–1865), like Tyrš was a German by birth, but became a Bohemian patriot and rejected the Greater German program to unify the Czech lands with a liberal German state. He was a man of profound culture, patriotism, and self-sacrifice, and a philanthropist for Czech causes. His given name was Heindrich, which he changed to Jindřich to stress his Czech identity. Tyrš and Fügner met in 1860, and realizing that they shared the same interests, they became friends. When Fügner and Tyrš spoke `together, it was mainly in German, because Fügner's Czech was considered "kitchen Czech" (Sayer, 1998, 109). Fügner helped Tyrš form the first Sokol club in Prague. He had traveled widely, was well educated in business matters, and helped his friend initiate the Sokol movement. He provided, at his own expense, a fully equipped Sokol gymnasium, and later financed a new building for Sokol. Fügner set a precedent for intelligent, unbiased leadership and devotion to the welfare of his people and country.

Fügner's unique contributions. Although Fügner died at the young age of 44, three years after Sokol was founded, he played a key role in the survival of the movement. Because he was effective in his political discretion, he spared Sokol from politics, and consequently government harassment. Fügner understood the authorities' concerns that Sokol gatherings could include political activities. He was successful in drawing outstanding men to the young Sokol organization, and was especially gifted in encouraging peasants, laborers, and artisans to join Sokol, because they were less likely to be involved in politics, and because he wanted diversity of Sokol membership. Fügner stressed the concept of social equality and viewed the Prague Sokol Club "as a means to up lift the downtrodden Czech masses" (Nolte, 2009, 1964). The equality of

members was underscored by addressing members as "brother," and the greeting "Nazdar" (to success) was derived from the Czechs efforts to raise funds for their National Theater. The term stressed the determination of the Sokols for their movement. His daughter, Renata, a writer, married Tyrš. Renata Fügnerová-Tyršova (1854–1937) became a role model for women, because she fought for their rights and the education of children. She was noted as a collector of art and a promoter of folk art, and for her design of the popular Czech Homestead *(Česká Chalupa)* illustration (Sayer, 1998, 120).

It was Fügner who introduced the red shirt of the Garibaldi Legions, as a component of the Sokol uniform. It was this brave group who defeated the Austrian army in Italy. This choice was his way of taunting the Austrian authorities, who could easily recall their defeat just a few years earlier (Nolte, 2009, 1964). The Sokol uniform consisted of loose trousers, high boots, braided jacket, and a hat with a falcon feather. With the opening of a new building, Sokol Prague was able to expand their offerings, e.g., by forming a library, a rifle group, and providing outings for camping and nature.

The Sokol Program

Tyrš' long-term leadership. Tyrš developed the Sokol movement's philosophy, which he detailed in two of his writings: "Our Task, Direction and Purpose" and "Elements of Gymnastics." He also launched a newspaper that included an article further defining his vision of the Sokol movement: "Our Task, Direction and Goal—a Sokol Classic of Principles." The formation of a Sokol Union was a dream not realized during the first two decades of the Sokol movement, despite Tyrš' attempts to obtain permission from the Austrian government to form such an organization. By 1873, he completed his examination of the Sokol purpose in an article "Gymnastics from an Esthetic Point of View," in which he asserted that gymnastics, at its best, is also art. His earlier writings addressed the roles of Sokol in hygiene, national economics, and the significance of gymnastic exercises. The value of Sokol gymnastic training for military readiness was also noted by Tyrš. For example, Sokol members served as guards for public events during the Austro-Prussian War in 1866. However, it was not until 1889 that the Habsburg authorities allowed the

Sokol Prague established in 1862 (photos circa 1890)

Jindřich Fügner (left) and Miroslav Tyrš

Renata Fügnerová, daughter of Jindřich Fügner and later, wife of Miroslav Tyrš

formation of a union of Sokol clubs, i.e. Czech Union Sokol (*Česka Obec Sokolská*). The Tyrš Sokol system was supplemented with gymnastic elements from other countries. American Czechs introduced rhythmic gymnastics, whereas, Indian clubs came from England, ladders from Sweden, and batons from France (Mahácek, 1938).

Tyrš remained at the helm of the Sokol organization until a short time before his death. The many responsibilities and activities that filled Tyrš' life affected his health. Thus, he went to a medical institution in Oetz, Austria, about twenty-five miles west of Innsbruck. On August 8, 1884, his body was found in the river; his death was due to drowning. Tyrš' legacy is clear: he skillfully chartered the club's ideological course and monitored the gymnastic program that he had developed, serving as its first physical director, and editor of the Sokol paper. Tyrš used the slogan: *"Co Čech to Sokol"* (Every Czech a Sokol) as a recruiting tool for Sokol membership (Nolte, 1993, 81). That Tyrš was truly a Renaissance man is evidenced by the several books that he wrote concerning art, his role as a promoter of the National Theater in Prague, and his work as co-founder of the Museum of Prague. He was also an elected member of the parliament in Vienna.

Tyrš in the Art World

A decade after founding the Sokol movement, Tyrš married Renata Fügnerová (Fügner's daughter) and began his service in art for the nation (Nolte, 1993). As noted earlier, Renata was active in the art world as a collector and promoter, thus she and her husband shared a common interest in art, as well as gymnastics. Tyrš' was keenly interested in inspiring a sense of Czech national art, and worked to call attention to Czech artists through lectures, displays, art clubs, and journals. Tyrš' viewed the work of the artist Josef Mánes, who designed the Sokol flag, as a model of Czech art. His goal was to lay down the ideological foundations for Czech culture. Additional information on Tyrš' taste in art and his philosophical interest in art is provided by Bažant (2011).

Growth of the Sokol Movement in the Czech Lands

Early Decades of Struggle

The Sokol idea took hold rapidly; formation of the first Sokol club in Prague was followed by nine additional clubs in Bohemia and Moravia during the same year, and a year later (1863) six more were established (*Památník Sokola Pražského,* 1883, 265). By 1883, there were 111 Sokol clubs in Bohemia and Moravia, with a membership of 12,602 men. These data reveal the depth of enthusiasm for the Sokol movement in the Czech lands. Not surprisingly, the Sokol banner accompanied Czechs who migrated to the US, and the first Sokol unit was formed in St. Louis in 1865, just three years after Sokol Prague was established. However, consistent growth of the Sokol movement in the Czech lands was hindered by the ruling classes in the Austrian Empire, who were not enthusiastic about democracy. In contrast Sokol in the US fit well with American democracy and tolerance, as exemplified by the Sokol philosophy. The Sokol falcon along with the Bohemian lion became a masthead and included the exhortations of "liberty, equality, agility, vigor, harmony, and courage." Over time it became evident that the Czech nationalism that grew during the mid-19th century was transformed into a mass movement by Sokol. The increases in the number of Sokol clubs and members are provided in Table 1. In 1882, the 1st National Congress was formed with 75 Sokol clubs in existence in Bohemia and Moravia (Garver, 1978, 117). The addition of more than 14,000 women members between 1902 and 1910 was associated with an 82% increase in the total number of members.

Political disputes and loss of members. Even though the monthly publication, *Sokol,* was launched in 1871, Sokol membership shrank from more than 10,000 in 1871 to just 7,191 in 1875 (Nolte, 2002, 102). In Moravia the authorities blocked Sokol projects and limited club activities. During the celebration of Olomouc Sokol's tenth anniversary in 1879, Tyrš detailed the problems of political dissent that, along with financial mismanagement and a lack of an adequate gymnastics program, caused many clubs to fail. Fortunately, Tyrš' two-hour speech occurred during a time when the Empire's government was seeking accommodation with the Slav population. Within one year, the number of Sokol clubs increased from seventy-one to eighty-six and more than 700 members were added. In 1881, the Sokol newspaper began publishing again and some younger members were added to the editorial board.

Sokol faces internal obstacles. The struggle for realizing Tyrš' dream of a Sokol movement experienced many obstacles during the early years, as exemplified by the power struggle between the Old and Young parties. Members of the former, while nationalistic, held the view that Sokol should keep its distance from politics. In contrast, the Young Czech party members advocated direct political involvement. Despite these disparate views, the determination of Sokol members was evident in the organizations motto, noted previously, *"Tužme se"* (let us harden ourselves). Following Tyrš' death in 1884, the evolving Sokol organization, *Česka Obec Sokolská (ČOS)* addressed issues regarding the goals of the movement and their clarification. The *ČOS* Congress considered work to be done and passed the St. Wenceslaus Resolution in 1895, so named because it occurred on the day honoring one of Bohemia's patron saints. The first goal was to expand gymnastic programs to make them available to more people, including the poor, to utilize more forms of exercise, and to educate people regarding the benefits of exercise. The second goal was to stress greater uniformity and discipline in the growing units. The third goal was to stress individual morality, and to include the club's nongymnastic work as well as physical training.

Jan Podlipný (1848–1914). This accomplished orator, lawyer, and Prague mayor served as the first president of *ČOS* from 1889 to 1906. He was known as a good organizer who established relations with American Sokols, which were of great importance in the eventual formation of Czechoslovakia. Podlipný led a delegation of Sokols to the second Olympic games in Paris and also brought Sokol gymnasts to France for competitions. He defended the Czech nationalists and socialists, a position that caused tensions within the organization. Podlipný tried to mediate a conflict between Hussites (a Protestant group that followed the teachings of Jan Hus) and Catholics, when the former wanted a statue of St. Mary removed prior to the placement of a statute of Jan Hus nearby. Podlipný noted that Hus was an admirer of Mary the Mother of God and suggested that the two statues were not in conflict. Unfortunately, this position led to his ouster as Sokol president, and he was replaced by Josef Scheiner, who had been Tyrš' assistant.

A challenge to Sokol principles. In 1904, Václav Kukán, a prophet of purification, demanded that "educational" work be on a par with gymnastics. He represented the Sokol organization in negotiations to fund a "Central Education Unit" for coordinating propaganda of Czech national organizations. He wanted to exclude veterans, Social Democrats, and German speaking Jews. Of course, his positions were in direct conflict with Sokol principles of inclusion and the avoidance of politics. Injection of politics again occurred with the rise of Social Democrats and Agrarian Parties. The former group formed the Workers Gymnastic Club, but most members aligned with the Czech National Socialist after the decline of the Young Czech Party and attacked Social Democrats as "Jews" and "Germans" opposed to the Czech cause.

Dr. Josef Scheiner (1862–1932). The task to reaffirm the traditional mission of Sokol fell on the shoulders of Josef Scheiner. A 1910 Congress reviewed the organization's identity and resolved that Sokol members should be aware that they are banned from using the club for political purposes. Such considerations were consistent with maintaining a purity of purpose for Sokol. From these events one can see that political agendas were frequently a threat to the organization. Scheiner was an effective leader, and after Tyrš' death, he was responsible, from 1887–1919, for editing Sokol publications and writing hundreds of editorials aimed at guiding Sokol programs. He also published the first biography of Tyrš and was the founder of the first instructor's school in Prague. Scheiner helped form *ČOS (Česka Obec Sokolská),* led Sokol into the International Gymnastics Federation, and during his leadership, Sokol clubs (units) were formed in all Slav countries. His courage is exemplified by his work during World War I as a leader of the Czech underground, during which time his activities were monitored by the Austrian police. In 1915, he was arrested and taken to Vienna to an infamous prison. Since none of the charges against him could be proved, he was released.

Dr. Jinřich Vaníček (1848–1914). Working with Scheiner, Vaníček promoted the Sokol movement as a component of everyday life. He served as *Náčelník* (Physical Director) and led the Sokol team at the Paris gymnastic competitions. Vaníček was a well-rounded athlete, who was interested in the military aspects of Sokol training.

Struggle for Women's Equality

Despite Tyrš' call for equality in his earliest writings, women struggled many years for full rights in Sokol (reviewed by Nolte, 1993). Initially their main role was to be supportive of the men's clubs and to help raise money. When they began training it was, in most cases, under the direction of men, using the men's system (Dusek, 1981, 96). However, in Prague, a group of women took the initiative to train women and girls. Thus, in 1869 the Gymnastic Club of the Ladies and Girls of Prague was formed, mainly by the efforts of three women: Sofie Podlipská, a novelist who became the first president, Kateřina Fügnerová, the widow of Jindřich Fügner, and Kleměna Hanušová, the daughter of a Czech Nationalist. Hanušová, Tyrš' pupil, made at least two innovations for women's gymnastics: she incorporated orthopedic exercises for girls (orthopedic gymnastics) and adapted the Tyrš system for women's needs. Even though women's emancipation was heralded by the Progressive movement of the 1890s, men resisted the idea of women attaining full membership in Sokol clubs. Usually women formed their own sections attached to men's clubs and by 1893 there were sixty women's sections with more than 2,000 members. An outcry from some men indicated their concerns were their belief that women tended to be jealous and class-conscious. However, in 1897, the *ČOS* charged all units to establish training sessions for women and adolescents.

In her paper about women in Sokol and Czech nationalism, Claire Nolte (1993), notes that despite the call by the *ČOS* for expansion of its membership to "All Czechs," it was reluctant to allow full participation of women. Much of this reluctance can be attributed to the conservative Austrian culture of the 19th century, which considered the main roles of women to be homemakers, raising children, and doing volunteer work.

Moravian women appeared to be more courageous in seeking equal status in Sokol than their Bohemian counterparts (Kabes, 2003). Progress was slow, but the number of women's sections of Sokol continued to increase. During the first decade of the 20th century, women made progress with the inclusion of rhythmic gymnastics and substantial growth in the number of women involved in training, but they still did not have equal representation in decision making. A resolution granting women full membership in Sokol was passed in 1914 and four years later women began directing their own gymnastic programs. This changing role of women corresponded to the Czech national movement and the increasing activism of Czech feminists in politics. Finally, in the 1920 Slet, fifty-eight years after the founding of Sokol in Prague, women marched as equals with men in the parade and were given authority over their own program (Nolte, 1993, 100).

Growth of Sokol Clubs: 1862–1912

Cervenka (1920) noted that during its first year of existence, Prague Sokol membership reached 1,000, and a total of eight clubs were established in the Czech lands. By 1902, there were 605 clubs in existence, and that number grew to 1,091 in 1912. Membership between 1902 and 1912 more than doubled from 50,238 to 119,183. Nearly one-third of the members were in Moravia/Silesia, which indicates that Sokol membership was proportional to the population of those provinces. Part of the large increase in the number of members was due to the first inclusion of women.

Sokol Organizations in the Czech Lands

ČOS was founded in 1889, and three years later the Moravian-Silesian Sokol organization was established. Then in 1896, the two groups united in the Czech Sokol Community. During World War I the Czech Sokols were disbanded but restored and renamed Community of Czechoslovak Sokols in 1920. This new organization became a single entity of all Sokols at home and abroad, apart from those in America (Jandásek, 1932). The Workers Gymnastic Organization, which split from the *ČOS* in 1897, was associated with the Social Democrats. Orel (Eagle) Catholic Gymnastic Association, founded in 1909, was based on the Tyrš system, but was relatively small, compared to the *ČOS*.

Sokol Becomes International

Sokol clubs are established outside the Czech lands. Formation of Sokol units in Slovenia (1864), the US (1865), Vienna (1867), and Russia (1870) were followed by those in Croatia (1874), Bulgaria (1879), and Serbia (1882). Numerous Sokol units were established in the US because of the country's dense population of Czech immigrants. Between 1865 and 1877 there were Sokol units in St. Louis, Chicago, New York City, Milwaukee, Baltimore, Pittsburg, Morrisania, New York, Cleveland, Cedar Rapids, Iowa, Detroit and Omaha. Some Sokol Women's units were established by 1869. The National Sokol Union, formed in Chicago in 1879, became the American Sokol Organization in 1917 when it was joined by District Fügner Tyrš and D.A. Sokols. Other Sokol organizations in the USA were established by the late 19th century: Polish Sokol in America (1887), and American Working Men's Gymnastic Association Sokol (1892). French gymnasts participated in the 19th century Prague Slets and a Sokol club was founded in Paris in 1892. The first Slovak Sokol club was established in Chicago, and in 1892 the organization became Slovak Gymnastic Unit Sokol (now Sokol USA), and then in 1905 the Slovak Catholic Sokol was formed. Sokols in America is the topic of Chapters 3 and 4.

Attempts to unite all Slavic Sokols. Following his election as president of the Czech Sokols in 1906, Dr. Josef Scheiner worked toward uniting all Slavic Sokols. In 1908, a year after the Sokol Slet in Prague, the leadership of *ČOS,* Slovene Sokol Union, and Croat Sokol Union met in Vienna and formed the Federation of Slavic Sokols. Subsequently, Russian and Serbian Sokols and the Galatian Polish Sokol Union joined the Federation followed by the Bulgarian Sokols. The Federation of Slavic Sokols was short lived because of a "troubled history, a testimony to the difficulties forging unity out of the diversity of the Slavic world" (Nolte, 2005, 126). One issue was the Czech's cultivation of the Russian Sokols, which alienated the Poles who then boycotted the 1907 and 1912 Slets. Another issue was the Bulgarian's displeasure that the Czechs had supported the Serbs in the second Balkan war (Nolte, 2005, 130–34). Despite the optimistic view of the federation's secretary that the Sokol movement would bring together all Slavs as brothers, the international organization did not last. As noted by Nolte (2005,

35), the Federation was based on "contradictions of Czech Slavism." Thus, the idea that Slavic solidarity via Sokol gymnastics could be realized failed because of: 1) international hostilities, and 2) significant differences in the histories of the various member nations.

The First Six Slets (Pre-Czechoslovakia)

The Slet concept. Data regarding Czech Sokol Slets is provided in Table 2. Public displays of physical exercise were not new to Tyrš, who had organized many for Prague Sokol. Thus, the first Slet (meaning a flocking of birds) was proposed as a means of demonstrating the beauty of mass calisthenics performed in precision, along with gymnastic competitions, theatrical events, and social functions. Slets, though not intended as political demonstrations, clearly displayed Czech unity and nationalism. The first Slet had been scheduled for 1868, but the newly formed Austro-Hungarian Dual Monarchy, forbade the parade or the recognition of a central organization; consequently, the Slet was cancelled. The Czech writer, Karel Čapek (1935), expressed the feelings of a spectator at a Sokol Slet when he witnessed the mass calisthenic performance of several thousand gymnasts:

> From those thousands, each individual earnestly and attentively enrolls himself to the total, until they are lost in the mass; here success is only that, that belongs equally to all. So it could be said, the ideal is coordination, accumulated and democratic strength. The desire is for voluntary discipline, for order functioning collectively and smoothly. Not drama, but order. Not combat, but cooperation. Not adventure but organization.

Slet I. Tyrš considered the occasion of Prague Sokol's twentieth anniversary as an opportunity for a "triumphant event" that would bring members together in a great all-Sokol festival. Accordingly, the first national gathering (Slet) was held in Prague in 1882, on Střelecký Island in the Vltava River, and included 720 men performing mass calisthenics, forty teams competing, and about 1,600 uniformed members marching in a parade behind Tyrš riding on a horse. Advanced gymnastic skills were demonstrated by Sokol trainers, and numerous celebrations with dancing and music were held. Also celebrated was the introduction of Sokol gymnastics in Czech schools. Toasts were raised for Bohemian and Moravian brotherhood and for Slavic solidarity. Even though the number of participants was fewer than anticipated, the spectators were awed by the exhibition and heard inspirational messages from speakers such as Edvard Grégr, who helped establish Sokol Prague.

Slet II. The second Slet, scheduled for 1887 in Prague, was forbidden in that city by the government, and limited competitions were allowed only in the city of Cesky Brod. American Sokols participated and won two second places in the competitions, which strengthened the bonds between the Czech and American organizations. Four years later, in 1891, the second Slet became a reality, and was held under the banner of the newly formed *Česka Obec Sokolská* (Czech Organization Sokol) and included participants from the US, Poland, Croatia, Slovenia, and France. This Slet was held on Královska Obora (now Stromovka Preserve) at the Vltava River. The growth of Sokol was clear when one compares the participants in this Slet (2,473) to the 720 that performed in the previous one, held in 1882. By now there were 229 Sokol Clubs and 24,000 members in the newly formed national organization. Importantly for the Sokol fitness model, nearly eight thousand of this group were participating in Sokol gymnastics. The Slet drew twenty thousand spectators, and 5,500 members marched in the parade.

Slet III (1895). Sokol's growth was clearly demonstrated, as evidenced by many encouraging signs. For the first time, about 700 juniors and boys performed on the field in an impressive display of youth. Mass calisthenics were performed by 4,287 men, who represented 346 clubs. Moreover, the gymnastic competitions included 439 teams. This Slet coincided with the Czech Ethnographic Exhibition in Prague, which was a huge success and helped publicize the Slet activities. Brotherhood was always a theme in the Sokol movement, and at this time was stressed, as indicated by movements of gymnasts performing in unison to commands, and by the fact that Sokol clubs were inclusive, and listed members of all occupations. The large scope of the Slet was such that it lasted four days. The number of spectators for this festival was estimated at 50,000 (Gajdos, et al., 2012).

Slet IV (1901). By the turn of the century, the uncertainty of the future and direction of Sokol had faded because the focus of the organization, i.e., gymnastics, had been reestablished with the educational mission falling under the responsibility of the club trainers and gymnastic directors. This move eliminated the development of two separate programs. This Slet, like those to follow, included a cultural tone, with the first event being an opera at the National Theater. For the first-time women, some 876, participated in a mass callisthenic exhibition. Mass drills were demonstrated by 6,705 men, an astounding increase of 1,500 men from the previous Slet. Moreover, this Slet was characterized by many international participants, including Poles, Ukrainians, Russians, Croats, Slovenes, Serbs, Bulgarians, Frenchmen, and Americans. This Slet was held in Letná Stadium, also the site of the next three Slets.

Slet V (1907). This gathering was under the direction of the newly formed Slav Federation and was characterized by an expanded program which lasted six days. The number of women participating tripled to 2,500 compared to Slet IV, and the number of men increased to 7,605. International gymnastic competitions were held for the first time, with the Czechs winning first place. The 100,000 seats in the stadium were filled and 15,000 members marched in the parade. Slovak Gymnastic Union Sokol, a newly formed organization in the US sent a seven-man team for the first time. The gymnastics competitions included low, high, and championship divisions.

Slet VI (1912). Called the "All Slavic Slet," this was the last such gathering before World War I. There were 30,000 Sokol participants, and the expanded stadium was filled with 125,000 spectators, as well as representatives from forty-five nations. Participants included 18,000 men, 5,650 women, 8,000 juniors and children. In addition to delegates and gymnasts from Bohemia and Moravia there were those from other Slav countries, e.g., Croatia, Montenegro, and from the US. Many writers and spectators commented that the Slets were characterized by the display of voluntary discipline, as well as precision of movement.

A year after the onset of World War I, Sokol was officially disbanded, but then reorganized with the creation of Czechoslovakia in 1918. Sokol during the First Czechoslovak Republic is the topic of Chapter 2.

Summary/Conclusions

The birth of the Sokol movement was a response of the Czech people's desire for an identity and nationhood. It came to fruition because a philosopher and visionary, Miroslav Tyrš, aided by his friend and colleague, Jindřich Fügner, recognized that fitness through a system of gymnastics could unify the Czech people and free them from the Austrian Empire and Habsburg rule. The Tyrš system stressed a sound mind in a sound body, brotherhood, and a moral character. The Sokol movement became international and endured many struggles, including the quest for women's equality. Most importantly, Sokol played a critical role in the founding of Czechoslovakia in 1918, because its members held leadership positions in the legionaries, a group of Czech and Slovaks who defected from the Austrian army and joined the allies. It was the future president of Czechoslovakia, Tomás Masaryk, a Sokol, who organized this fighting force. It was the record of this legendary army that played the key role in gaining support for the new nation. The importance of Sokol in the lives of Czech immigrants and their future generations is evident from the efforts of Czech settlers in America in establishing Sokol clubs, and is the topic of Chapters 3 and 4.

Left: Postage stamp honoring Josef Scheiner, who led the Sokol movement from 1887 until 1919. Right: Statue of Miroslav Tyrš outside Tyrš House (headquarters of the Czech Organization Sokol) in Prague.

Sokol gymnasts with the movement's founder Miroslav Tyrš (pointing in back row)

Left: Early Sokol flag with a Sokol motto: Tužme se (let us harden ourselves)
Right: Women marching onto the field at the 1907 Sokol Slet in Prague

2

Sokol in Czechoslovakia's First Republic

Characteristics of the New State

Formation of the New State

"During the spring and summer of 1918, the Allied governments committed themselves to support the program of the Czechoslovak National Council in Paris" (Korbel, 1977, 32). On October 28th of that year the Czechoslovak National Council in Prague proclaimed the independence of the new state of Czechoslovakia, and in January 1919, the Paris Peace Conference approved the establishment of the Czechoslovak Republic. The new nation included Bohemia, Moravia, Silesia, Slovakia and Ruthenia with a total population of more than 13.5 million, and with 70–80 percent of all the industry of the Austro-Hungarian Empire, as well as 17% of the Hungarian industry that had been developed in Slovakia.

Sokol and the Legionnaries

As discussed in Chapter 1, Czechoslovakia was established largely because the legionnaires persisted in their efforts as freedom fighters, in response to the leadership of Tomáš Masaryk, who recruited so many Sokols and others for the cause. The bravery and determination cannot be overstated. One of the greatest legacies of the Czecho-Slovak Legion is their epic march across Siberia. This feat underscores the legionnaires fight for democracy, which President Wilson, in 1919, called their "brilliant record" (McNamara, 2016, 322–3). "The first financial support for the resistance movement came from Sokol funds" (Lejková-Koeppl, 1968, 1473). Masaryk and Beneš (who succeeded Masaryk as president) affirmed the role of Sokol education in the formation of the legionnaries by eliciting the discipline and patriotism that was essential in the formation of the Czechoslovak Legions. Many of the legion's elite were Sokol leaders. The Sokol "nazdar," became the greeting used by the legionnaries. "When the revolution came and Czecho-slovakia was proclaimed an independent state, there were Sokols who, with the utmost zeal, undertook he task of acting as guardians of the security of the people. They disarmed the Austro-Hungarian troops and achieved a successful revolution without any bloodshed" (Lejková-Koeppl, 1968, 1473). "It is very well known that the Sokol units in America, Canada, England, and elsewhere supported leaders like Beneš, not only with moral, but with material help as well. The American Sokols, especially, contributed substantially to the liberation of Czechoslovakia" (Lejková-Koeppl, 1968, 1474).

Development and Growth of the New Nation

Czechoslovakia seemed to reflect the ideals of post-World War I, including a strong democratic flavor (Dimond, 2007). These characteristics were consistent with the views of the president, as well as foreign minister Edvard Beneš, who also served as Deputy Chairman of the League of Nations. The ties to the West were understandable, considering the support of the US in creating the new state and Masaryk's friendship with and support from US President Wilson. Moreover, both the US and Great Britain represented the democratic values to which the Czechs and Slovaks subscribed. Although, these ethnic groups had been two large components of the Austro-Hungarian Dual Monarchy, they had their own identities and political agendas. The merging of the two historical groups was for tactical reasons, i.e., their unity was a basis for breaking up the monarchy, as a means of realizing the goal of self-determination.

Post-World War I progress was impressive. By 1937 there were thirty-seven universities in the new republic, compared to only one in 1920, and there were now two independent, reputable independent newspapers: *Lidové Noviny, and Prager Tagbatt* (Korbel, 1977, 64). The nation's independence fostered a "cultural renaissance" that was evidenced by a "great creative ferment" (Korbel, 1977, 66). Theatre, music and fine arts flourished, and writers such as

Čapek, and the composers Leoš Janáček and Bohuslav Marinů became internationally renowned.

Sokol Thrives in the New State

Reorganization of Sokol

Adapting to new conditions. The most urgent talk regarding the new country was "to form new lines of action in harmony with the changed conditions of a liberated country" (Jandásek, 1932, 76). The movement stressed that it was a national program, and according to Sokol teaching, brotherhood was to come into the new state as a zeal for social justice. In accordance with President Masaryk, the Sokol Congress in 1924 affirmed that "Every loyal, truly conscious Sokol shall be a defender of the Republic and our democracy, and as such a political and social worker in it" (Jandásek, 1932, 77). It became clear during the post-World War I years, that Sokol was a leader in both physical fitness and politics. In 1930, the Czechoslovak Sokol Organization had 352,888 members of which 25% (56,376 men and 34,829 women) were participating in physical training (Jandásek, 1932, 66–7). At that time participation in the gymnastics program was required of all young people. During the post-war years more clubs acquired their own training facilities; by the early 1930s, 27% owned their gymnasiums. Other active clubs continued using space in local halls or schools. During this decade, swimming and camping activities were also stressed.

Sokol and Slovakia. With the formation of Czechoslovakia, the unification of the Czechs and Slovaks was not without difficulties. "The Slovak's outlook on life was different to that of the Czechs, and in particular it was unlikely that the Sokol's Hussite imagery would be well received in Catholic Slovakia" (Dimond, 2007, 192). One must remember that Sokol was a Czech movement under Austrian, and later, Austro-Hungarian rule, whereas Slovaks were ruled by Hungary, where Sokol was recognized only after the end of World War I (Jandásek, 1932, 67). Although Ivan Branislav Zoch, a teacher who led his students in "Slovak awareness" and taught physical fitness as early as 1866, Sokol clubs did not appear in the 19th century. A Sokol in Žilna was founded in 1908, but establishment of other Sokol clubs usually failed. In 1912, the Hungarian Government refused to approve an application for Sokol clubs in Slovakia. Thus, except for a few clubs, established illegally, Sokol did not exist in Slovakia prior to the founding of Czechoslovakia. Consequently, Slovak Sokol membership was only about 12,000 in 1919. As Czech neighbors and fellow Slavs, Slovaks understood the value of the Sokol philosophy, but they were not part of the long-lasting Czech Organization Sokol *(Česka Obec Sokolská)* that became the Czechoslovak Sokol Organization *(Čechoslovenská Obec Sokolská)* in 1920. Thus, they joined a movement that had its own fifty-eight-year ethnic history, and well-established programs with many participants. Not surprisingly, Sokol membership in Slovakia grew slowly during Czechoslovakia's first decade.

Sokol youth in Czechoslovakia. In 1930, 73,305 junior boys and girls (aged 14–18 years) and 199,943 children under the age of fourteen were participating in Sokol activities (Jandásek, 1932, 66). Clearly, it was the large increase of youth participation that spurred the growth of Sokol during the first seventeen years of the new republic. Unlike Sokol's early years, which began with participation of men exclusively, then later men and women, in 1937, 50% of Sokols were eighteen years of age or younger (Dimond, 2007, 192–3). As seen in Table 2, this age group accounted for only 25% of the participants in the 1920 Slet, but in the 1938 Slet they comprised 63% of the participants. These data support the conclusion that Sokol was convincingly establishing a youth movement.

Growth of Gymnastics and Physical Fitness

Sokol's role in competitive gymnastics and school physical education. Marie Provazníková (1890–1991), a revered leader of *ČOS* from 1932–1938, and the 1948 Olympic women's gymnastics director, was elected head of the Federation of International Gymnastics in 1946. During an interview (Jaros, 1992), she discussed some historical milestones of Sokol in her country and noted the importance of Sokol in establishing physical education programs in the schools as far back as the late 19th century. Moreover, the *ČOS* had schools for training instructors with various levels of expertise (degrees). These schools graduated thousands of teachers who taught not only in Sokol

Sokol members in a small town in Bohemia pose for a photo (circa 1920).

Tyršův dům (Tyrš house) transformed from older structures after World War I. It is a facility that houses Sokol head-quarters, the organization's history and functions as a training center.

gyms, but also in schools and the military. Tyršův Dům (house, or building) was opened in 1925 to house the *ČOS* headquarters and Instructor's school. The facility featured a large gymnasium, swimming pool and a summer practice area. Provazníková successfully promoted the expansion of gymnastic competitions, as well as those of other sports. One generally unknown story is how the balance beam was standardized by Sokols. Although the beam was in use for many decades prior to the establishment of the first Sokol, the width of the beam was decreased to ten cm, its height standardized, and descriptions of beam routines were published. German gymnasts came to Prague to see the modified beam and learned the published routines; their women's gymnastics team then won the gold medal in the 1936 Olympics.

Sokol expands its programs. Jandásek (1932, 66), in his paper on the Sokol Movement in Czechoslovakia, notes the post-World War I growth of *ČOS* programs and membership. Most importantly, a total of 276,248 juniors and children were active in the Sokol gymnastics program. There were 22,118 male and female instructors, who were certified by completing instructor training programs and who understood the Tyrš system and philosophy. Various commissions were established for different aspects of Sokol programs, e.g., swimming, canoeing, fencing, medical exams, and scientific investigations. Specialized schools trained leaders for other activities, e.g., theatrical productions, puppet exhibits, and choral productions. These schools provided more than 560 new instructors each year (Jandásek, 1932, 70). Educational activities were more extensive with the establishment of Czechoslovakia, as indicated by the fact that in 1931 there were 12,600 lectures and 7,200 excursions available. Many specialized periodicals were published, the oldest of which was the monthly *Sokol,* a journal founded by Tyrš in 1871, that dealt with gymnastic theory and practice. Administration was the topic of *Věstník Sokolský* (Sokol Herald). Four other monthly publications dealt with 1) male instructors, 2) female instructors, 3) lectures regarding Sokol, and 4) regeneration.

Other Czech Sokol societies. A gymnastic Catholic organization, Orel (Eagle), analogous to Sokol had 112,629 members in 1930 (Jandásek, 1932, 66). The Association of Workers Gymnastic Units, which also utilized the Tyrš system of gymnastics training along with Social Democratic Party principles, listed 64,221 members.

Sokol Plays a Role in Czechoslovak Politics

At the end of the war in 1918 "Sokol volunteers were given arms and were posted as guards at military establishments and ammunition stores" (McNamara, 2016, 301) because of their physical training. This event affirmed Sokol's status in the new nation. By 1920, Sokol membership had reached 562,657 (5% of the population) (Příručka, 1978). These impressive numbers underscored Masaryk's vision of Sokol as a force in developing a Czech ethnic core to help maintain its demographic position in the new country, and eventually helped elect more Czechs to government positions. At the same time Masaryk subscribed to the concept of six ethnic groups (Czechs, Slovaks, Hungarians, Ruthenians, Poles and Jews) contributing to Czechoslovak patriotism. Of these six groups, Czechs were the largest, followed by Slovaks, whereas the other four groups constituted much smaller populations. Thus, one can appreciate that the Czech dominance would not be an asset for ethnic unity. Moreover, there were differences between Sokol members regarding the organization's philosophies. Tyrš had stressed a nationalist identity and inclusion of military elements, whereas, Fügner's focus was on social equality (Dimond, 2007, 193). The early post-World War I increase in new Sokol members was mainly due to their alignment with Fügner's philosophy of social equality, rather than a need of militaristic training. This is understandable considering that the Czechs were no longer ruled by the Austrian-Hungarian Dual Monarchy.

Sokol and nationalism. In his discussions regarding Sokol's role in Czech nationalism between the two world wars, Dimond (2007, 193) notes that the political outlooks of Masaryk and Tyrš were complimentary. Sokol was intended to be a moral example to the Republic that was currently embracing both national passions and Communist intrigue. Masaryk offered ideological pillars: peaceful nationalism, parliamentary democracy, social reform, and resistance to clericalism. The Sokol Plenary Congress of 1924 supported moderate politics by rejecting Communist doctrine and banning fascists from the organization. Yet ethnic nationalism continued to be a theme aimed at reversing the effects of "Germanization and

Hungarianization" (Jandásek, 1934, 12–20). Because the Sudeten lands were now part of Czechoslovakia, Germans living there did not benefit from Sokol's task of developing a Czech ethnic core (Dimond, 2007, 191–2). Determined to maintain their German identity, they promoted the Turnverein Gymnastic Society and used the organization for Sudeten German party politics. In the 1930s Sokol membership increased for several reasons. One of which was the support of the popular president Masaryk, and another was the popularity of the gymnastic program. The third was Sokol's association with a Czech identity. So emblematic had Sokol become of the nation that there were proposals to rename the currency "sokol" (Sayer, 1998, 177). Understandably, another important factor that helped increase Sokol membership from 704,185 in 1932 to 818,188 in 1938 was the Nazi threat.

Slets in Czechoslovakia 1920–1938

VII. Slet (1920). The first Slet held in a Free Czechoslovakia, consisted of a five-day celebration, preceded by three Sundays of activities. It included the participation of 50,566 men and women, 19,612 juniors and 13,180 boys and girls. The Slet opening was attended by President T.G. Masaryk and 60,000 spectators in Letna Stadium, while Prague citizens enjoyed the site of 36,000 marchers parading through their city. This Slet was the first in which women, took command of their participation, and in which junior girls participated. For the first time, a mass drill display by 4,800 older men was included in the program. The economy of the post-World War I nation was struggling, but the idea of postponing the event was rejected. Although economic and political problems limited the participation of some foreign countries, the American Czech and Slovak Sokols sent a delegation of 650 men and women, and Great Britain and France sent large numbers of "outstanding personalities" (Havlíček, 1948, 34). Fifty male and female gymnasts from Sweden were enthusiastically welcomed. Havlíček concluded that the Slet "fulfilled its mission: it mobilized the moral forces of the nation for the task of reconstruction and convinced observers from abroad that the new Czechoslovak State was democratic, healthy and vigorous."

VIII. Slet (1926). Enthusiasm for the Sokol Movement was clearly demonstrated by the spectators who filled the newly built Strahov Stadium's 135,000 seats. The Slet's activities filled 17 days and included 103,026 participants, and for the first time the number of women (34,402) outnumbered the men (18,925). The number of foreign participants was the highest in Slet history. Thus, long after Tyrš' death his mantra: "every Czech a Sokol" was nearly realized. Over 2,000 train trips carried over one million passengers into Prague; street cars carried 1,200,000 passengers in one day. The 13,888 juniors and pre-juniors that participated indicated the sharp increase in young people involved in Sokol gymnastics training, as they accounted for more than 50% of the participants. The Slet days also included many cultural programs, e.g., plays and opera.

IX. Slet (1932). A year earlier the Slet was promoted by a Sokol Relay Race featuring the carrying of the Sokol flag from nine border points of the Republic by runners. Held in Strahov stadium with a capacity for 180,000 spectators, the Slet accommodated the post-World War I increase in the number of participants, with more than 130,000 exhibiting their fitness skills. The field accommodated 17,000 gymnasts performing in unison. In addition to the 60,016 men and women participating in the festival, 26,121 juniors and 44,104 children demonstrated their skills. A record number of 65,328 persons marched in the five-hour parade. Again, there was an impressive number of countries that participated, which strongly affirmed the international respect for the Sokol movement. This Slet also included particularly impressive demonstrations of advanced gymnastic skills, as well as competitions in other sports, e.g., decathlon, pentathlon, and fencing. Moreover, other offerings also included the arts: sculpture, painting, musical composition, singing, and drum and bugle corps. A Tribute to "Tyrš' Dream" was created and staged with special attention to artistic values.

X. Slet (1938). With German troops concentrated at the borders of the Czechoslovak Republic, the 10th All Sokol Jubilee was scheduled to be held under the slogan: "For freedom and Democracy." Most impressive at this ten-day Slet, was the number of young participants. There were about 20,000 boys and girls under the age of ten, 41,600 aged ten to fourteen, and 33,700 juniors. Men and women who participated totaled 62,181 of which 33,581 were women (Dusek, 1981, 157). Similarly, more junior girls than junior boys participated. Competitions in addition to gymnastics included track and field, swimming, wrestling, weight lifting and fencing. The US delegation of Czech and Slovak Sokols numbered 135. The parade featured 60,640 Sokols with 665 flags. The total number of spectators, over the ten-day event, was estimated to be one million. Among them were representatives of 30 foreign countries (Gajdoš et al., 2012). This was the last Slet before the Nazi occupation a year later.

Sokol's Role in the Sport of Gymnastics and Physical Education

Initial Opposition to Gymnastic Competitions

Sokol objections. Tyrš regarded gymnastic competition as an important means for the "activation of gymnasts" (Kössl, 2003, 12). Moreover, he even compared the first Sokol Slet to the Great Greek Olympic Games. Some Sokol leaders who emphasized the physical education aspects of the movement, regarded sport to be narrow, and one instructor in 1882 wrote an article condemning sport for its "one-sidedness, international character and educationally detrimental influence" (Kössl, 2003, 13). Not surprisingly, this attitude resulted in some young people leaving Sokol and joining newly established sports clubs. A year before the modern Olympic Games were revived, an article in the Sokol journal, *Borec* (22.05, 1895) stated: "We do not regard as desirable to support participation of our Sokol gymnasts in those competitions." Such objections were based on the international nature of the Olympics and the emphasis on performance, which were not consistent with the Sokol's focus on various types of exercise and patriotism.

Struggle for Olympic participation. Dr. Jiří Guth, who was recognized as a Czech representative to the International Olympic Committee, stressed the importance of the Olympic Games, and began negotiating with representatives of Sokol and other sports organizations. He wrote to Pierre de Coubertin, who was re-establishing the Olympic Games, that the participation of the Czechs in the Olympic Games "without our gymnasts—the Sokols—would be very incomplete" (Kössl, 2003, 15). However, the Czech Sokols were not alone in their reluctance to send gym-

nasts to the Olympic games, because gymnastic associations of other countries initially refused to participate. An occasional Czech gymnast did compete in the games: one in 1900, two in 1908 and one in 1912. Participation of Czechs in any sport was problematic because the Austro-Hungarian monarchy objected to independent Czech Olympic participation, even though the Czechs had their own Olympic Committee (COV), founded in 1899. Attempts to "liquidate or at least limit the Olympic independence of the Czechs and Hungarians" failed because the head of the International Olympic Committee rejected the monarchy's claim that 'Bohemia is a mere Austrian province" by responding that there is "athletic autonomy within a country" (Kolár and Kössl, 1994, 11–2).

Sokol and the Olympic Games

The formation of a Czech Olympic Committee occurred because it became more evident that participation in international competitions were beneficial for a Czech identity and recognition (Kolár and Kössl, 1994, 11–12). Dr. Jiří Guth continued his struggle for the recognition of Czech athletes. Those who competed in Olympic Games were recognized for their skills, "thus Czech Sport, the Olympic movement and the Sokol movement all helped boost the national consciousness of young sportsmen" (Kolár and Kössl, 1994, 14). Guth was finally successful in gaining some recognition for the Czech athletes competing in the 1912 Olympic Games. They were identified on a list of Austrian athletes with the abbreviation, COT, indicating the "Czech Olympic team" (Kolař & Kössl, 1994, 13). They were also allowed to wear the Czech emblem. By this time the Czech Olympic Committee had established a firm position in Czech sport and gained the support of Sokol officials. With the establishment of the Czechoslovak Republic, all state and legal barriers were eliminated, and as discussed in the next section, Sokol gymnasts won numerous international awards.

Czech and Czechoslovak Sokols Develop Competitive Gymnasts

Sokol became an early member of the European Gymnastics Federation (EGF) in 1897, which in 1920 became the International Gymnastics Federation (FIG). Sokol gymnasts participated in international gymnastics competitions as early as 1889, when the first *ČOS* president led a delegation of Sokols to Paris where three Sokol gymnastic teams won three first places (Havliček, 1948). During the first half of the 20th century Czech Sokol-trained gymnasts won many medals in international competitions. In the World Championships, Sokol men's teams were first in 1907, 1911, 1922, 1926, 1930 and 1938, and second in 1934. They placed second in the 1928 Olympics. At the first World Championships in 1934 that included women, the Czechoslovak women's team won first place, a feat that they repeated in 1938 (Příručka, 1978). In the Olympic Games the women's team placed second in 1936 and first in 1948. The 1948 US women's team, which placed third, included Sokol New York's Ladislava (Ladie) Bakanic.

Individual Olympic gymnastics medals. In the 1924 Olympic Games held in Paris, members of the Czechoslovak Men's Team won four silver and three bronze medals. The first gymnastics Olympic gold medal was won by Bedřích Šupčík in the rope climb event. At the 1928 Games (Amsterdam), Czechoslovak gymnasts won one gold, one silver and one bronze medal. An Olympic high point occurred in the 1936 Olympic Games in Berlin when Alois Hudec performed a very difficult routine to win the gold medal in the rings event. Hudec had recovered from polio and became an outstanding gymnast.

Individual medals at World Championships. At the first World Championships (Prague, 1907) the gold and bronze medals in the all-around event were won by Czechs. Medals for individual events were not awarded until 1930. The success of the Sokol-trained Czech male gymnasts in the all-around event continued: 1909, silver; 1911, gold; 1913, gold and silver; 1926, silver and bronze; 1930, silver and bronze; 1938, gold and silver. When medals for individual events were added (for the 1930, 1934, 1938 World Championships), eleven additional medals were won by Czechs. Alois Hudec, the 1936 Olympic champion on the rings, also won the event at the 1934 and 1938 World Championships. In addition, he was the silver medalist on the horizontal bar and parallel bars in the 1938 World Championships. One of the most successful Czech Sokol female gymnasts was Vlasta Děkanova, who was world all-around women's champion in 1934 and peaked at the 1938 World championships by winning five gold medals: all-around, beam,

vault, parallel bars, and team. In the men's competition at the 1938 World Championships Jan Gajdoš won three gold medals: all-around, floor, and team. Gajdoš competed in four World Championships, spanning twelve years (1926, 1930, 1934, 1938), and won the silver medal in the all-around event in 1930.

Sokol System in Physical Education

Tyrš encouraged incorporation of other training modalities within his system of training, and encouraged his followers to explore other varieties of apparatus for utilization in Sokol training. Thus, not surprisingly after his death in 1884, the use of Indian clubs, an English invention, and ladders from Swedish gymnastics were common in Sokol gymnasiums (Macháček, 1938, 80). Such additions expanded the scope of physical education programs. As noted earlier in this chapter, the Sokol system of training was introduced into schools in Bohemia as early as the late 19th century. Instructors for school physical education programs, and for military training were educated in Sokol schools. Štěrbova and Vlček (2015), in their review, indicate that physical education was introduced as a compulsory school subject by 1870 with the goal of helping "school children to gain skillfulness, confidence and courage and to enjoy order." In the late 1870s the physical education program, which emphasized discipline, included floor exercise, marching, and apparatus was defined as gymnastics. These activities and goals clearly reveal Sokol's influence in the school system; some elements of the Ling Swedish system and a few games were also included. In the 1920s the Tyrš Sokol system continued to comprise the core of the physical education curriculum. Novel ideas were incorporated into the Sokol program and thus into the public-school system. Augustin Očenášek attended the International Congress of Physical Education in Paris, where he learned about the value of rhythm during physical exercise and became dedicated to the idea of combining music with calisthenics (Dusek, 1981, 249).

Because Sokol instructors came to Serbia, as well as to other Slavic countries, in the late 19th and early 20th centuries, Sokol gymnastics became well ingrained in the culture (Vukašinović, et al., 2017). Accordingly, gymnastics was the most important school exercise program, and was introduced into Serbian elementary schools as early as 1868. Similarly,

Sokol training played a major role in physical education programs in Croatia (Škegro and Čustonja, 2014). The introduction of gymnastics as a required course for teacher training colleges occurred in 1875. The Sokol system was implemented following the earlier influence of the German Turnverein in Croatia.

Sokols under Nazism and Communism

Bohemia and Moravia became a Protectorate of the German Reich in 1939, whereas Slovakia opted to gain independence from Czechoslovakia. The appointment of Reinhard Heydrich, Chief of German Security Police, in September of 1941 as Governor of the Protectorate, considered a part of the Greater Reich, sent a shock wave of terror through the Czech population. Heydrich was charged with the "Final Solution," the plan to murder Jews in Europe, and within three months of his appointment Protectorate courts sentenced 342 people to death and turned 1,289 over to the Gestapo police. Thirty-four thousand Czechs were deported to death camps. Heydrich's focus of terror was on the educated populations, and cultural groups, especially Sokol (Krejci, 1990, 160), which was banned on October 8, 1941, a month after he took office. Many Sokols were active in the resistance movement and helped in the assassination campaign ("Operation Anthropoid") of Reinhard Heydrich (Dimond, 2007, 194). On May 5, 1942 he was assassinated by Czech parachutists who were trained in Great Britain. A Sokol underground unit was also involved in the assassination as well as hiding the parachutists in a Prague church. Their actions resulted in an intensified terror campaign causing the deaths of more than 50% of pre-war Sokol leaders.

It is estimated that approximately 23,000 Czechs were executed by the Nazis in retaliation for the Czech's assassination of Heydrich (Korbel, 1977, 163). Because of their participation in the resistance movement, many Sokol members were sent to Terazin, a concentration camp near Prague and then to Auschwitz. According to Burian (2015, 1–2) between 1939 and 1945, 11,611 Sokols were imprisoned, 1,120 were executed in concentration camps, and 2,176 died in prison. One of those who died in Auschwitz was Dr. Stanislav Bukovský who succeeded Josef Scheiner as president of the Czech Sokol Organization. A key contribution of Sokol Revolutionists was that they provided an apparatus, on a massive scale, for the resistance movement.

The importance of Sokol to a Czech nation was underscored by Edvard Beneš' message, in 1942, to Czechs under Nazi occupation. He stated that "it is not possible to imagine the development of our nation without the Sokol, without Sokol thinking" (Dimond, 2007, 86).

Between Fascism and Communism

Josef Korbel (1977, 218–252) describes the brief post-war period when the citizens of Czechoslovakia experienced both hopes and fears for their future. Due to their World War II experiences they were soundly antifascist and the new government outlawed fascist organizations. National unity was compromised when German and Hungarian minorities were "deprived of citizenship and their property confiscated if they were unable to prove their political reliability—and very few of them could" (Korbel, 1977, 220). The presence of the Red Army during the first six months following the war was also an ominous factor. The Communist Party began to infiltrate various departments, most notably the Ministries of Agriculture, and Interior, and they instituted a well-organized propaganda campaign.

By 1947 the bureaucracy, economy and the press were largely under Communist control, and featured a campaign of Marxist ideals. The Party claimed to be the "sole heirs of all the finest and best in the national tradition from the Czech kings in the Middle Ages to the distinguished life of Masaryk" (Korbel, 1977, 232). They also called for a "class struggle," praised the meaning of Christmas, and suggested friendly relationships with the West. The fact that the cold war was intensifying placed Czechoslovakia in a tenuous position. Aided by their deceptions and a campaign of intimidation, the Communists used a coup to takeover the government on February 25, 1948. Because of this change in government, "a new stream of refugees started arriving in America, among them a large proportion of students and teachers, journalists and professional people" (Laska, 1978, 58). In the spring of 1948, the American Fund for Czechoslovak Refugees was established with the goal of resettling thousands of refugees.

Sokol Emerges Briefly after World War II

Sokol's focus in the first Czechoslovak Republic had been the preservation of a Czech identity in the country's German-dominated Sudeten land. However, following the Nazi occupation, President Beneš expelled Germans from this region. This move was supported by many Sokol members who were grieving the loss of so many Sokol leaders that were involved in resistance groups (Dimond, 2007). One of Sokol's most admired leaders, a physician named Stanislav Bukovský a gymnast and coach and successor to Dr. Scheiner, died in a concentration camp in 1943. Antonín Hřebík served in a resistance group and was imprisoned in Auschwitz, but survived and became active in Sokol at the end of the war. Nevertheless, Beneš' action came to be viewed as ethnic cleansing. In 1946, the Sokol revival began and included establishing units in the border lands vacated by the Germans. However, despite the Czech's animosity toward the Germans, most Sokols favored membership for children of Czech-German marriages. Despite the weakening of Sokol by the war, the activity of its members resumed spontaneously, and by 1947 Sokol claimed more than one million members (Burian, 2015, 1–2).

The Communist challenge. Tyrš emphasized democracy in the Sokol Movement and stated that "democracy alone can ensure the essential balance and harmony in human society" (Havliček, 1948). He wished that democracy would be firmly established through Sokol, as an ideal among the Czech people. However, between 1946 and 1948, the Sokol emphasis on democracy was challenged by both Czech and Slovak Communists who promoted the notion that Masaryk's values and that those of Sokol were comparable to those of the Communists and the organization supported the Communist's two-year plan to put Czechoslovakia's economy back on sound footing. This idea was initially accepted by some of Sokol's socialist-leaning members, but when Stalin overruled Czechoslovakia's right to discuss economic aid with the US, Sokols were again drawn to democracy, which was a pillar of the organization (Dimond, 2007). The idea of "Slavism" began to lose creditability with the realization that Moscow, not Sokol, was leading eastern European culture. The Communist take-over was systematic, as the Party members penetrated key government positions at all levels. By 1947 most committee chairmanships were held by Party members (Korbel, 1977, 225–6).

Slovaks and Sokol. In 1945, Slovak Sokol was technically illegal and Sokol members feared reprisals by the authorities. The Sokol publication, *Sokolský Věstník* implored members in Slovakia to describe their contributions to the uprising against the Nazi sympathizers (Dimond, 2007). But Czechs began separating themselves from Slovaks. Despite the similarities of Czechs and Slovaks, there are important differences between the two ethnic groups. First, Slovaks had been under Hungarian rule, while Czechs were ruled by the Habsburgs of the Austrian Empire. Second, the Sokol movement had a clear-cut Czech identity. Finally, the merging of Czechs and Slovaks into a Czechoslovak Republic was a necessity, rather than an ideal. After the creation of Czechoslovakia, in 1918, about 18,000 Slovaks were Sokol members and that number grew to only 32,00 by 1935 (Dimond, 2007).

Sokol is incongruous with Communism. By 1948 Sokol was dissolved in eastern Europe, (except in Czechoslovakia), because nationalism was considered an enemy of Communism. However, the 1948 Slet was an issue the government could not outwardly attack, because the event was a strong statement of the importance of Sokol. Meanwhile, Sokols demonstrated heir resistance to the incoming communist dictatorship by stressing their devotion to the legacies of Masaryk and Beneš (Burian, 2015, 2). That same year the women's Czechoslovak gymnastic team competed in the Olympic Games in London, led by their legendary ČOS National Director of Women, Marie Provazníková. She had fallen into disfavor with the Communist Government because of her strong support for Sokol ideals and her unwillingness to allow the Communists to infiltrate and dominate the ČOS (Dusek, 1981, 376–79). However, the fifty-seven-year-old Sokol leader, declaring that freedom in her country was lost when Czechoslovakia joined the Soviet bloc, defected and became the first political refugee in Olympic history. The Czech women's team won the Olympic gold, which stood as a great tribute to Provazníková and the Sokol movement. Once the 1948 Slet ended, the Communist government assailed the Sokol organization more aggressively by printing a photo of Josef Stalin on the cover of the last issue of the *Sokol Věstník* (Dimond, 2007, 205). Finally, in 1952, the organization was incorporated into a body called "State Committee for Physical Education and Sport." Thus, "it became clear that the Sokol had definitely ceased to be a democratic organization and had become a helpless tool of the Communist regime" (Gajdoš, et al., 2012, 12). Communist party members dominated the Sokol Executive Committee, and subsequently thousands of Sokols were arrested. The Czech and Slovak people's disappointments with the Communist Coup of 1948 were clear: "by 1950 some 100,000 persons had left their country" (Dubovický, 2003, 49).

Summary/Conclusions

Considering the important role that Sokol played in the formation of Czechoslovakia, Sokol then became the guardian of the new republic. It was in step with the republic's first president, Tomáš Masaryk, who was a long-time Sokol member. He helped the acceleration of the Sokol movement which added many more participants, especially the youth. Sokol thrived under the democracy, and served as its partner. The Sokol system was adopted in the schools, even in other countries. Champion gymnasts emerged from the Sokol ranks, some became world and Olympic champions, e.g., the women's team in 1948 won the Olympic gold in London. However, Sokol was a threat to governments that resisted democracy and freedom, thus the organization was banned by the Nazis and the Communists and many Sokol leaders were imprisoned and even executed. Sokol faced many challenges between 1920 and 1948, but still made historical contributions to fitness, gymnastics, freedom and democracy.

Slet VII in 1920, the first in the newly established country, Czechoslovakia.

1926 Slet in Prague's newly constructed Strahov Stadium:
Man competing on the rings (top photo) and an estimated 14,000 junior girls performing mass calisthenics (bottom photo). The Strahov Stadium accomodated 135,000 spectators at the time. The area of the field was 73,984 square yards, which is equal to the area of eleven American football fields.

1938 Czechoslovakia's men's world gymnastic championship team (left),
and vault performed by Jan Gajdoš all-around gold medalist.

Alois Hudec, 1936 Olympic champion on the rings event.
All photos on this page are from Czech Organization Sokol.

Top: *Men performing calisthenics at the 1938 Slet in Prague.*
Below: *Thirty thousand men participated on the field at the same time. Photos from Czech Organization Sokol.*

1938 Slet: women performing mass calisthenic drills.
Photo from Czech Organization Sokol.

Mass calisthenic performances at a 1948 Slet: Women (top photo) and pre-junior and junior girls (bottom). Top photo by Karel Šmirous, bottom photo by Czech Organization Sokol.

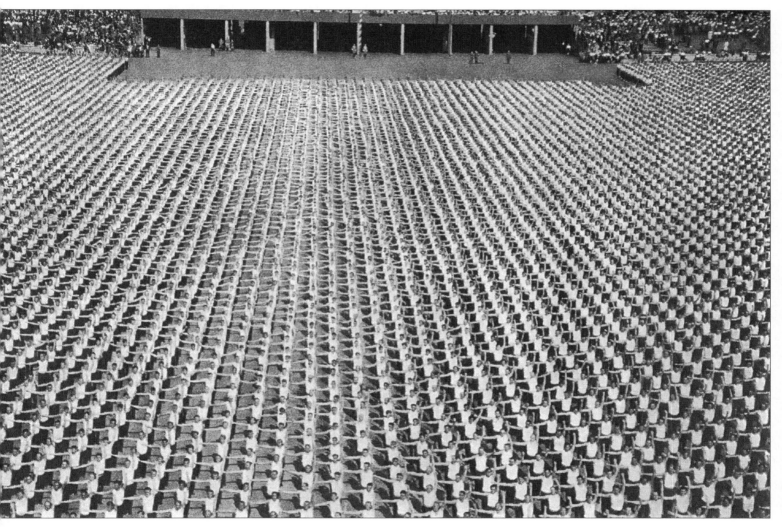

Men and junior boys performing at a 1948 Slet.
Photo by Karel Šmirous

*1948 Olympic women's gymnastics team champions, Czechoslovakia (top),
and women performing with clubs at 1948 Sokol Slet. Photos from Czech Organization Sokol.*

Gymnastic instructors course participants (circa 1923).

3

Czech-American Sokols: A Transatlantic Journey

Introduction

Czech immigrants were part of a wave of settlers from Europe during the late 19th and early 20th centuries, and with them came their dreams, language, and customs, including Sokol. They settled on farms, and in small towns and cities, where they formed communities and raised families. Like other ethnic groups, the Czech settlers had an impact on American life, including values, work ethic, and civil responsibility. Although Czech settlers assimilated, they also continued to value their culture, which most often centered around the Sokol clubs they founded. Czech settlers were emboldened with the spirit of adventure in America, which offered them opportunities denied in their "old world." This chapter includes the Czech immigrant story, as well as the development of the Sokol movement in America and its influence on Czech-American culture. It addresses the origins of Sokol clubs and the formation of national Sokol organizations, whereas Chapter 4 focuses on the individual Sokol clubs (units). Sokol's contributions to gymnastics in North America is the topic of Chapter 5.

Early Czech Immigrants: Founders of Sokol Clubs in America

Historical Background of Czech Immigrants in America

Motivation to emigrate to the USA. Czechs made the transatlantic journey to the United States in the hope of freedom, better living conditions, and, in many cases, the opportunity to own land. Many of the men also did not want to serve in the Austrian army and fight for causes that were not their own. The Czech's hope of some independence within the Austrian Empire faded with the establishment of the dual monarchy, i.e., the Austro-Hungarian Empire.

These factors caused an increase in the number of Czechs migrating to the US in search of independence and various opportunities, of which democracy was a prime motive. The immigrant's hope was summarized in 1930 by the President of the American Slav Congress: "Arriving at their destinations and taking possession of the land they spent all their efforts to secure a decent standard of living and to lay the foundation for a family hearth around which their future young generation could gather" (Zizka, 1943, 144). The Czech immigrants learned about life and opportunities in America from friends and relatives who had settled there, and who sent them newspapers (written in Czech) and letters detailing their own experiences.

Settlers adapt to life in America. One of the surprises that the Czech immigrants found in their new land was the loss of life and destruction of cities caused by the Civil War and its lasting effects on American society (Jožák, 1998, 152–3). The settlers still harbored thoughts about the struggle for political democracy during the revolutions of 1848, when their hope for some form of self-government faded.

Early settlers. The first Czech to settle in America was Augustine Herman in 1633; a century later Moravian Brethren established a settlement in Georgia and then in Pennsylvania (Dubovický, 2003, 11). However, it was not until the second half of the 19th century that significant waves of Czechs immigrated to the USA. "The foremost gateways for entering the United States were New York, Baltimore, New Orleans, and Galveston" (Dubovický, 2003, 18). Many of the earliest settlers were farmers and settled in the Midwest and Texas where farmland was plentiful. The Homestead Act of 1862 offered 160 acres to anyone willing to work the land for at least five years. "Czechs were among the first pioneers to transform the wilderness and prairies into arable land and clear forests for new settlements" (Dvornik, 1961, 92). However, after 1890 more Bohemian and Moravian migrants were from cities, compared to those from rural areas. This shift occurred because a severe 1873 economic depression caused farmers in their Czech homeland to move to the cities where they learned the skills of factory workers, and consequently fit into the urban workforce. Although, some of the settlers were unskilled laborers, many were skilled: blacksmiths, tailors, shoemakers, carpenters, barbers, shop keepers, town clerks, bookbinders, cigar makers, button makers, cooks, artists, and actors (Svoboda, 1993, 12).

Emigres to the cities after 1900. Early 20th century Czech settlers favored the urban areas, because many were skilled workers or professionals (Biroczi, 2003, 11; Stavařová, 2009, 33). Since schooling opportunities were good in their homeland, 97% of Czech immigrants from the Dual Monarchy in 1910 were literate, compared to 66% of all Slav groups (Balch, 1910, 479). A segment of the Czech immigrant population also consisted of intellectuals, journalists, writers, composers, and physicians. Such credentials enabled the advancement of the Czech-American communities. The history of Bohemia and Moravia documents the high intellectual power of the Czech people, as indicated by their extensive literature, advances in science, and the founding of the first university in the Austrian Empire, established in Prague, by King Charles IV in 1348.

Czech Settlements in America

The number of Czech immigrants increased steadily from 1861 to 1910. Hanzlik (1970) lists the numbers of immigrants from Bohemia and Moravia by decades. Between 1850 and 1870 only 56,132 Czechs immigrated to the USA, whereas, during the next two decades that number was two-fold higher (Figure 2). The largest number of Czechs (94,603) entering the US occurred between 1901 and 1910. Following World War I, fewer Czechs immigrated to the US for at least two reasons. First, they were part of their own country (Czechoslovakia was established in 1918). Second, US immigration policy was stricter after World War I.

Advantages of Settlements. Czech immigrants formed their ethnic communities for several reasons (Svoboda, 1993, 113). Foremost was mutual protection and a better life. Second was the preservation of culture, as facilitated by a common language, social interest groups, festivals, and in many cases, common goals. Thus, the Czech-American setting provided the

newcomers both security and social satisfaction. As summarized by Svoboda (1993, 115): "Czech customs prevailed. People spoke Czech, danced to Czech music, cooked Czech dishes, and read Czech newspapers." Sometimes Czech emigres settled near Germans or Poles, so they could more easily communicate (Jožák, 1998, 151).

Early Czech settlements. Although New York was the main port of entry into the USA, one of the earliest ports of entry for Czechs migrating to America was Galveston, Texas, and many, particularly Moravians, who came to that port, settled in various Texas towns. As detailed by Bicha (1970), numerous Bohemian and Moravian emigres were early settlers in Wisconsin where they found inexpensive land, low taxes, and liberal residence requirements. They were also attracted to the good soil and sources of wood for building log cabins. The first two settlements with a large Czech population were Racine, and the farming town of Caledonia later called Tabor (Dvornik, 1961, 47). Manitowoc, Wisconsin, opened the Bohemian Opera House in 1885, which was maintained by *Západní Česko-Bratrská Jednota* (Western Bohemian Fraternal Association) and *Slovanská Lípa,* and utilized by Sokol for gymnastics, assemblies, lectures, and dances (Laska, 1978, 32). However, immigration to Wisconsin had decreased, already in the 1870s, whereas more settlements then occurred in other farming states, e.g., Iowa, Nebraska, Minnesota, Kansas, and the Dakotas. The 1900 US census lists 155,640 European-born Czechs and 199,939 American-born Czechs. The number of Czech immigrants "is likely higher than those listed here, because before 1881, and even after that year, many Bohemians and Moravians were listed as Austrians" (Chroust, 2009, 1). Figure 3 illustrates the distribution of Czech immigrants in 1900, by states with the highest percentages. The height of Czech immigration was between 1901 and 1910 when 94,603 Czechs immigrated to the USA (Hanzlik, 1970). By 1914, there were about 500,000 Bohemians and Moravians who had settled in the US (Chada, 1981, 23). At that time Illinois' Czechs numbered 124,225, while Nebraska and Ohio each had about 50,000, followed by New York, Wisconsin, and Texas with Czech populations between forty and fifty thousand. Chicago's Czech population of 110,736 was third in the world, behind Prague and Vienna. Other

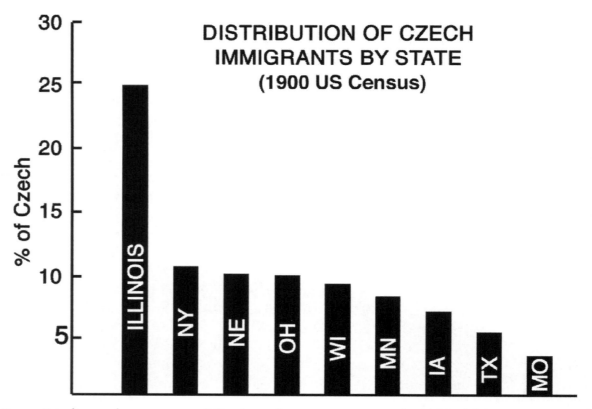

IMMIGRANTS TO USA FROM CZECH LANDS
1861 - 1914
(Based on data from J. Hanzlik, 1970)

- ● Total for Decade
- ■ Highest One Year Number

Number of Immigrants / Decade

100,000
7,500
5,000
2,500

} Data is for 3 years

1861-1876 1871-1880 1881-1890 1891-1900 1901-1910 1911-1914

Figure 2. The number of immigrants from the Czech lands settling in the US is illustrated. The data indicate a steady rise in the number of settlers. The number peaked during the first decade of the 20th century.

DISTRIBUTION OF CZECH IMMIGRANTS BY STATE
(1900 US Census)

% of Czech

30
25
20
15
10
5

ILLINOIS NY NE OH WI MN IA TX MO

Figure 3 indicates the percentage of Czechs settling in various states by 1900. Of the nine states with the greatest number of Czech settlers, seven are in the Midwest (New York and Texas are the exceptions).

US cities with significant numbers of Czechs were (in order), New York, Cleveland, St. Louis, Baltimore, Milwaukee, Omaha, and St. Paul. These figures likely do not reflect the actual number of immigrants who settled in the US, rather they show the number of persons living at the time of the census.

Texas Czechs. The first Czech settlement occurred in 1847 (Laska, 1978, 7), however, the major influx of Czechs into Texas came some fifty years later, which resulted in 41,080 Czech immigrants residing in Texas in 1910, virtually all of whom were original settlers, rather than those transplanted from the Midwest or East Coast (Chroust, 2009, 80). Most immigrants from Eastern or Southeastern Moravia, were from towns such as Vsetín, Místek, and Frenštát (Dvornik, 1961, 59–60). They tended to settle on farms in the fertile counties between Dallas, San Antonio, and Houston. There were about 250 Texas Czech communities in the early 20th century (Machann and Mendl, 1983, 42). Many settlers were adherents of the Catholic faith, in contrast to the many Freethinkers in the north. Moreover, Moravians were more persistent than Bohemians in retaining their traditions and customs (Chada, 1981, 25). The draw to Galveston as a port of entry was enhanced by steamship companies and land agents who "advertised Texas to Europeans" (Machann and Mendl, 1983, 20). One 1910 ad stated that "Galveston was the best port of entry because custom agents were less strict there." Czech settlers started arriving in Dallas around 1910.

Migration of Czechs to the farm states. Many of the Czechs who came to America before 1900 were owners of small farms or were farm laborers who saw the opportunity to own land. Since the best opportunities were in Iowa, Nebraska, Kansas, and the Dakotas, the new immigrants settled in small communities or helped develop them. Saline County in southeastern Nebraska, particularly the towns of Wilber and Crete, received many settlers from other states, especially from Wisconsin; they arrived as early as the 1860s (Bicha, 1970, 198). Sometimes the new small towns were given names of towns in the Czech Lands, e.g., Vsetín, Velehrad, Hostyn, and Praha in Texas, Pisek in North Dakota, Protivin in Iowa, and Tabor in Minnesota, and in South Dakota. Like immigrants from other countries, the Czechs who settled on farms faced uncertainties, and in the prairies, isolation and loneliness were common. However, in communities with an adequate number of settlers, they were able to embrace their love of music, dance, various celebrations, and social life. Even small communities typically had a benevolent lodge, and in some cases drama societies. Life in these communities was strengthened by the close family ties, characteristic of Czech culture. Thus, these small communities survived and even thrived.

Czech arrivals in New York. Many Czechs entered the US during the last several decades of the 19th century via New York, and those that settled there could succeed if they had resources to establish a business, or had a skill that was in demand (Biroczi, 2003, 8). The principal settlement was in Manhattan between Second Avenue and the East River from 65th to 78th Streets (Čapek, 1921, 20). Many found work as cigar makers in a company started by a group of Czech immigrants (Stavařová, 2009, 34), and others introduced the pearl button industry to New York. Opening a tavern in a Czech neighborhood, in New York or other US cities, was welcomed by the locals, because it was a meeting place, a place for making contacts and conducting business, and it served as a social setting and reminder of the Czech home. "Beer was brewed there, Czech songs were sung, Czech dances, especially polkas, were danced, and overall the Czech-American taverns functioned like their counterparts in the Czech lands" (Stavařová, 2009, 35). Other smaller Czech settlements were established in the Morrisania section of the Bronx, Winfield, Corona, College Point, Binghamton, and Yonkers. In 1921, the Webster Branch of New York City Public Library had 15,000 volumes of Czech books, the largest collection in the US (Čapek, 1921, 51).

The Czecho-Slavic Association, founded in 1850, was the first Czech organization in America. Its purpose was the support of poor immigrants and the promotion of national activities (Habenich, 1961, 104–105). It was short-lived, but was followed by the formation of many fraternal and benevolent organizations, e.g., *Slovanská Lípa* (Slavic Linden), as well as the first trade union in 1870. One of the most prosperous and famous Czech newspapers, *Slavie*, was established in 1862 and provided brief outlines of services available in the Czech community. In 1864, *Včela* (honeybee) was founded and in 1867 became Sokol Gymnastic Unit in New York, a club regarded as the "most excelling" of New York's associations (Habenich, 1966, 106). Sokols organized musical comedies, dramas, balls, and choral performances. Numerous social, cultural, educational, and benevolent organizations were founded in New York in the mid-19th century. In 1896, the Bohemian National Hall was built on East 73rd Street, under the patriotic motto *Národ sobě* (a nation unto itself). Despite New York being a major port of entry to the USA, in 1870 there were only 1,456 Czech settlers in the city compared to 2,656 in Chicago (Dvornik, 1961, 28–29). Midwestern Czech settlements were facilitated by the availability of rail service as early as 1852 from New York to Chicago, making the westward journey relatively easy.

Czech settlers in Chicago. With the influx of skilled workers and professionals, most immigrants began settling in urban areas, where there were many employment opportunities. Most had the specific skills needed in these communities, and already in 1866, the first Czech labor organization was founded in Chicago. "From 1861 on, the Czechs of Chicago began to manifest a lively social and national activity, the center of which was the national organization *Slovanská Lípa* (The Slavic Linden Tree) founded in 1862" (Dvornik, 1961, 30). It did not take long for Czechs to own businesses, including banks, and building and loan associations. In the 1920s, Chicago Czechs controlled fifteen state and federal banks and more than 50% of the assets of building and loan associations (Biroczi, 2003, 9). Home ownership was higher for Czechs in Chicago, as well as in Cleveland, than for other ethnic immigrant groups (Chada, 1981, 35). Life in cities offered a greater variety of lifestyles and more educational and social opportunities. Moreover, immigrants living in cities could select a specific church denomination, social club, or employment that more closely fit their training or background.

As detailed in his Ph.D. thesis, Horak (1920, 15) noted that by 1920 there were over 200,000 Czechs in Chicago, due largely to the surge of immigrants arriving during the first decade of the 20th century. Immigrants living in entirely Czech neighborhoods, such as those in Chicago, preferred shopping in Czech-owned shops and many gathered in Czech pubs to socialize (Fornůskova, 2009). In addition to the common language spoken in these shops, the prices were usually lower than those in stores outside the community (Horak, 1920, 34). The expression and preservation of Czech culture was facilitated by Czech intellectuals, journalists, professors, educators, and politicians. However, immigrants in such self-sufficient communities were slower in learning English. Horak (1920, 21–26) described the various early settlements in Chicago, the first of which was south of Lincoln Park in 1852–1855. Some other early Czech neighborhoods included "Plzeň" (Pilsen), "Czech California," *"Malá Jižní Strana"* (little south side), Town of Lake, and then the suburbs of Cicero and Berwyn, as well as Brookfield, Stickney, Riverside and Oak Park (Dvornik, 1961, 31–32).

Czech settlers in Cleveland. Significant Czech settlements began in the 1860s, and in 1867 Cleveland Czechs established the singing chorus, *Lumir* (Habeneich, 1996, 499), and St. Wenceslaus Church (Sabo and Alzo, 2009, 10–15). In this parish the Union of Czech Catholic Women of America was organized in 1879 (Dvornik, 1961, 45). The heart of Cleveland's Czech community was known as *Zizkov*. Other neighborhoods were also given Czech names, e.g., *Vršku* (on a hill), *Praha,* and *Svoboda* (liberty). *Slovanská Lípa,* established in 1862, was the oldest association in Cleveland, and featured a drama club, but became extinct in 1877 (Habenicht, 1996, 499–502). The city was home to many benevolent and fraternal societies, Sokol clubs, and two educational societies, both of which had libraries. A key development for the Czech community was the construction of the Czech National Hall, completed in 1897. By 1920, Cleveland's Czech population reached 43,997 (Čapek, 1926, 26). Two Czech weeklies, *Pokrok* (Progress) and *Dělnické Listy* (Worker's Paper) were published in the 1870s, and a decade later Cleveland also had two Czech dailies. (Habernich, 1966, 502). Most of Cleveland's early Czech settlers were from the Bohemian towns of Pisek, Prague, and Tabor. Later, in the early 20th century, migrants from Holešov in southern Moravia settled there. The development of the Czech community in Cleveland, including settlements, organizations, publications, and culture was detailed a century ago (Ledbetter, 1919).

Czech settlers in other major cities. Large Czech communities also developed in other Midwestern and Eastern cities; listed here are the number of Czechs in other American cities in 1920 (data from Čapek,

1926, 626–31): New York 43,839, Omaha 11,463, Baltimore 8,694, St. Paul—Minneapolis 6,434, and Detroit 4,519. Of cities with populations fewer than 100,000, Cicero, Illinois, was home to 13,205 Czechs. In Cedar Rapids Iowa, with a population of 32,811 in 1910, about 26% were Czech, and the city had established a Czech Village by 1900 (Habenich, 1966, 27). Formation of Sokol clubs was a high priority of Czech immigrants, which most often included the various artistic groups, e.g., theater, choral groups, bands, and dance groups. By the 1920s two-thirds of the Czech population lived in large cities (Biroczi, 2003, 11).

Czech Culture in and Contributions to American Life

Newspapers and journals. Many factors served to preserve Czech culture in America, one of which was Czech language newspapers and magazines. Already in 1860, two Czech-American newspapers began publishing: *Národní Noviny* (National Gazette) in St. Louis, and *Slovan Amerikánský* (American Slav) in Racine, Wisconsin. The two newspapers merged a year later and became *Slave,* with Karel Jonáš as editor (Biroczi, 2003, 32). Edward Rosewater, with Jan Rosický, launched the *Omaha Bee* newspaper and the *Pokrok západu (Progress Westward),* a serial publication. Rosický also published *Květy Americké* (American flowers) and *Hospodář* (Homesteader). A group of Midwesterners formed the Bohemian American Committee, and in 1892 began publishing the *Bohemian Voice,* a monthly journal with the goal of providing the Czech view regarding the conflicts in the Habsburg Empire (Chroust, 2009, 1). Thomas Čapek (1861–1950) and Jiří Král (1870–1951), two young immigrant editors with law degrees, edited the publication. A comprehensive newspaper series on Czech settlers in Nebraska and Kansas was published by Frank Mareš in Omaha's *Hospodář* in 1891–1895. The publication *Svoboda* (Liberty) was owned by August Haidušek, a La Grange, Texas banker, and jurist.

Books. Immigrant's homeland memories were kept alive by books such as Anthony Dignowity's *Bohemia Under Austrian Despotism,* the first (1859) English language work about Czechs in Austria, and probably the first book on Czech immigrant life published in America. It featured an open discussion regarding events and progress of the 19th century, as the author detailed his early life memories. Willa Cather's novel, *My Antonia* (1918), captured the spirit and hardships of immigrants in the plains of Nebraska and the life of a Czech girl. Thomas Čapek, was a prolific writer of Czech immigrant history. His works culminated in the 1920s with two encyclopedic books: *The Czechs (Bohemians) in America* and *Nasé Amerika* (Our America) (Chroust, 2009, 19). Some other books on immigrant life included a comprehensive work by Antonín Houšt regarding American immigrant parishes in 1890, and Joseph Čada's books on Czech immigration and Czech immigrant radicalism (Chrust, 2009, 20–21). These, and other, publications kept the Czech immigration history alive.

Fraternal and benevolent societies. These groups played important roles for Czech immigrants by providing Czech-speaking lodges, insurance policies, supporting various groups, and paying benefits to members in case of illness or death. The Czech-Slovak Protective Society came into existence in 1854 as *Česko-Slovanský Podorújcí Sponečnost (ČSPS),* and in 1870 the *Jednota Českých Dam* (Unity of Czech Ladies) was founded. Western Fraternal Life originated as *Západní Česko-Bratrská Jednota/ZČBJ* (Western Czech Fraternal Organization) in 1897. Another early organization was Bohemian Citizen's Benevolent Society (1892) in Astoria, New York. By 1920, membership in Czech fraternal and other societies was 123,183 (Čapek, 1920, 263–264).

Some notable artists and scientists. Czech culture in America was emboldened by Antonin Dvořák's service as Director of the National Music Conservatory in New York (1892–95). His famous composition, the *New World Symphony,* was a portrayal of life in America. This contribution brought Czech cultural expression to Americans of all ethnicities. Interest in Dvořák's work also opened the doors to other composers, especially Bedřich Smetana's operas and later the music of Bohuslav Martinů (Dvornik, 1961, 98). Another notable visitor was Nuevo artist Alphonse Mucha (1866–1952) who lectured in Chicago and Brooklyn and spent seventeen years in America (Dubovický, 2003, 31). A famed Czech classical pianist and composer, Rudolf Friml came to the US in 1906 and joined the Curtis Institute in 1939. Albin Polášek (1879–1965), a Moravian who immigrated to the US when he was twenty-two, became an award-winning sculptor and played a key role in supporting Czech causes. The scientist, Ales Hrdlička (1869–1943), was a renowned anthropologist who became assistant curator in the Smithsonian Institution. During both World Wars, Hrdlička "placed his contacts and prestige in scientific and political circles at the service of Czechoslovakia" (Dubovický, 2003, 45).

Czechs in politics. Some Czech immigrants or their offspring were interested in politics as an avenue to serve their country and at the same time advocate for Czech interests. John Wilkes Kiter, of Pennsylvania was one of the earliest Czech-Americans elected to Congress (in 1791), and then reelected four times (Čapek, 1940). Subsequently, he became a US Attorney for the Eastern District of Pennsylvania. His son Tomás was elected to Congress in 1826. Some others who served in Congress were Anthony Michalek of Illinois (1905), Tomás Knop of Wisconsin (1911), John Baka of Ohio (1929), and Karl Stefan of Nebraska (1934, 1936, 1938). Wisconsin's Karel Jonáš was elected to the state senate in 1883, and then elected Lt. Governor in 1890. The Czech-born American Anton Cermak, a Sokol member, became Chicago's mayor in 1931, but was assassinated in 1933 while accompanying President Franklin Roosevelt. During the first half of the 20th century, Berwyn, Illinois, boasted seven Czechs mayors. Roman Hruska of Omaha, a life-long Sokol and son of a Czech immigrant, served four terms in the US Senate (1954–1976).

Adolf J. Sabath, a US Congressman for forty-seven years from Chicago, introduced the first workman's compensation bill, the first old-age pension plan, and the US Congress resolution "acknowledging the right of the Czech lands to freedom and independence" (Dubovický, 2003, 32). Louis Brandeis (1856–1941), a son of Czech immigrants, became a US Supreme Court Justice and helped Masaryk obtain American support for the formation of Czechoslovakia. Chicago's Otto Kerner Sr., also a son of Czech immigrants, was a federal judge from 1939–1952. Many Czech immigrants or their offspring were elected to state legislatures, as compiled by Čapek (1940).

Czech contributions to education. Czech language schools were founded by the mid-nineteenth century in Milwaukee (1862), Chicago and Cleveland (1864), New York (1865), Cedar Rapids (1869), and later in many other cities and towns. In 1887 the monks of St. Procopius Abbey in the Czech Pilsen neighborhood in Chicago established St. Procopius College, which is now Benedictine University with its main campus in Lisle, Illinois. Today this institution is keeping Czech culture alive by partnering with Palacky University in Olomouc, Czech Republic. In Chicago, the Czech immigrant Dr. Frank Jirka was a member of the Board of Education (1890–1891) and Jaroslav Zmrhal served as Superintendent of Public Schools in 1921.

The Czech-American Subculture: Welcomed in America

Czech immigrants and the social order. Czechs viewed America as the "land of opportunity," a view especially contrasted by their limited opportunities in the Austrian and Austro-Hungarian Empires. As the evidence reveals, Czechs, as a group, were notably successful in adapting to the new life and land, and were most resourceful in grasping opportunities. They built communities, and while promoting their culture, they also began to assimilate. Although, culturally homogeneous, they were diverse in talents, education, religion (or non-religion), and politics. This diversity was a strength that enabled the development of communities, and contributed to American culture, economy, civic life, and social structure. Joseph Chada (1981, 226) noted the success of Czech-American immigrants:

> The Golden Years of Czech ethnic life extended from late 1890s to the early 1930s. By the mid-1910s this Czech-American subculture had attracted the attention of the average American, who recognized the economic achievements the Czechs had attained in their urban and rural communities, as well as their successes in cultural, political, and civil matters. Finally, the average American appreciated the great effort the Czechs had exerted in their pursuit of a national ideal in World War I—that of political sovereignty for Czechoslovakia.

The Czech work ethic and loyalty were applauded by J.D. Rockefeller in 1870, who employed many Czech immigrants at Cleveland's Standard Oil Co.

(Dvornik, 1961, 42–43). However, resistance to immigrants was evident during World War I, and for some time after, as a strong Americanization movement took hold. Finally, the advocates of the resistance realized that "eradicating from the hearts and minds of immigrants all memories of their native land" was not possible (Laska, 1978, 119). Thus, it became clear that these law-abiding citizens could not be expected to put aside what was of such value to them.

Czech values. Zizka (1943, 138–139) wrote: "The cultural contributions of the Czechs of America were so numerous and of such value that they were found quite sufficient in their relationship to the social order of the New World (thereby) becoming its integral element." The moral values of working-class Czech immigrants were evident. Zizka then notes that they tended to be satisfied with little material goods, were patient in their poverty, and had an innate sympathy for family, health, and a rather well-developed national solidarity. "These moral values fitted the American milieu very well," and were observed at a time when the foundations of civilizations were being established by pioneering immigrants. The artistic contributions (e.g., Czech Folk Art, music, and theater) were also timely, as late century America had little classical tradition its own. The music, art and dances were full of life and color and called attention to the artistic contributions of the Czech settlers" (Zizka, 1943, 138–139).

Rural communities. In describing the Czech communities of the late 19th and early 20th centuries Zizka (1943, 100–103) notes that in rural regions of Nebraska and Texas the Czech communities are "so well integrated," their agricultural enterprises "so well developed," in addition even second and third generations used correct Czech speech. Rural Czechs knew their candidates for office, often personally (and many of them were Czechs); the rural social milieu was such that members of other language groups assimilated into the Czech community. In these rural towns, Czechs were usually in the majority.

Urban communities. In contrast to the rural settlements, those in the cities were more integrated and had their own local daily press and a variety of fraternal, benevolent organizations, social groups, churches, and meeting halls. Urban immigrants were more likely to integrate earlier. Thus, while sharing common culture and language, rural and urban settlements differed.

Sokol as a Cultural Immigrant Center

Histories of the various Sokol clubs (known as "units") validate their roles as facilitators of Czech-American culture, a topic included in Chapter 4. Sokol Halls were not limited to the gymnastic and fitness goals of the organization, but provided meeting places for fraternal organizations, various cultural clubs, choral groups, lectures, Czech language classes, and theater. They often included a library, and hosted bazaars for various cultural and charitable causes. Chada (1981, 142–143) concluded that Sokol's "program of physical fitness, social and cultural activities, and, above all, a highly charged ethnic spirit, attracted both sexes." Therefore, "Sokol became an integral part of social and national life." Moreover, Sokol was ethnically focused and assertive; in its gatherings, such as Slets, it demonstrated its dedication to ethnic, cultural, and national goals.

Czech-Americans and World War I

A chance for Czech independence. The quest for nationhood for the Czech people was, without question, dependent on a breakup of the Austro-Hungarian Dual Monarchy. Masaryk, the future first president of Czechoslovakia, sought financial support from Czech and Slovak Americans, and had discussions in this regard with the Czech Sokol President, Dr. Josef Scheiner (McNamara, 2016, 81–82). Already at the onset of World War I in 1914, an organizer of a rally in Chicago predicted that the war would bring down the empire. Demonstrations against Austro-Hungarian rule of Bohemia and Moravia occurred in many US cities. The Czech National Alliance was formed by the representatives of Sokol, CSPS, the Czecho-American National Council, and the Czecho-American Press Bureau. Fund-raising bazaars in Cedar Rapids, New York City, Omaha, Cleveland, and Chicago provided over $500,000 for the cause of Czech independence (McNamara, 2016, 81); then on Thanksgiving Day in 1918, a nation-wide campaign collected $320,000 (Čapek, 1920, 263–4). Subsequently, the Bohemian National Alliance raised hundreds of thousands of dollars annually by imposing a tax on member's dues. These funds were used at the end of the war in 1918 to purchase food for war victims in their homeland. More than one-million dollars was donated by American Czechs and Slovaks for their countrymen abroad. When the US entered the war in 1917, 50,000 young men of Czech descent volunteered their service. Sokol clubs played a key role in these fund drives, because so many of their members were immigrants or their children.

A dream realized. It was through the efforts of Tomáš Garrigue Masaryk, a Moravian by birth, his Bohemian colleague, Edvard Beneš, and the Slovak astronomer, Milan Rastislav Štefánik, that Czechoslovakia came into existence at the end of World War I. This opportunity occurred because of the demise of the Austro-Hungarian Dual Monarchy, and recognition of the Czechoslovak National Council as a de facto government. Another key to this development was the Czechoslovak Legions of Allied Forces, which underscored the Czech and Slovak people's determination for self-rule.

Immergence of Sokol in America

St. Louis: First Sokol Club (Unit) in America

In their new homeland, Czech settlers were freer to promote their ethnic pride than were the countrymen they left behind. St. Louis was an early destination for Czech immigrants who established a strong sense of community, as evidenced by the establishment of the first Czech Catholic church and the first Czech Benevolent Society (*Česko-Slovanský Podorújcí Sponečnost* or CSPS) in America in 1854. Just four years later, the Czech-American periodical, *Národní Noviny* (National News), began publication, and an educational and cultural organization, Slavic Linden was established. Not surprisingly Czech immigrants were committed to promoting their culture, which included forming Sokol units. Thus, in 1865, just three years after the appearance of the first Sokol unit in Bohemia, the inhabitants of St. Louis' Bohemian Hill established the first Sokol unit in America. These immigrants were aware of Tyrš' teachings and announced that a meeting would be held within two weeks. Enthusiasm for a Sokol club in St. Louis was evident at that meeting, as sixty-five men in attendance applied for membership, and the new Sokol unit was declared to be a "progressive organization" (Nolte, 2011, 76). An executive committee was formed, and a gymnastics director was appointed, but it was necessary to utilize various locations for gymnastics training, since a

permanent location was not available until 1890. Women began training in Sokol St. Louis in 1876.

Despite the enthusiasm for the first Sokol in America, there were problems during Sokol St. Louis' early years. Two of the unit's founders, Karel Proháska and Jaroslav Vostrouský left the St. Louis area in 1866, and a cholera epidemic struck the community that same year. Their departure created a leadership void, and gymnastics classes were hindered by a lack of, or inadequate facilities at make-shift locations. Thus, during the early years there were no records of gymnastic activity. Ten years after its formation, Sokol St. Louis was reorganized.

Other Early Sokol Units in America

Between 1866 and 1873, nine Sokol units were established. The first of these was *Tělovičina Jednota Sokol v Chicagu* (Gymnastic Unit Sokol in Chicago). In 1867, New York's "Czech cultural *Včela* (honeybee), transformed itself into a Sokol club" (Nolte, 2011, 77), and another club, called Svornost was formed in Morrisania (Bronx), New York. Then, other Sokol units were established in Milwaukee (1868), Perun in Cleveland (1870), Blesk in Baltimore (1872), and Tyrš Cedar Rapids (1873). Nine more Sokol units appeared between 1875 and 1880 from New York to Nebraska: Budivoj (Detroit), Fügner (Long Island, New York), Omaha, Cechie (Chicago), Czech-American (Kewaunee, Wisconsin), Czech-American (Manitowoc, Wisconsin) Czech (Cleveland), Pilsen (Chicago), and Wilber, Nebraska. Table 3 lists the forty Sokol units that were established by 1892. They were in New York, Maryland, Ohio, Michigan, Wisconsin, Illinois, Iowa, and Nebraska.

The need for community centers. As noted earlier, Czech settlers brought their customs with them to America. Many of them, e.g., choral, dance and theater, were often components or affiliates of Sokol. Formation of Sokol units were a priority because 1) they provided fitness programs as well as a social center for families, 2) other Czech groups often met there, and 3) Czech school classes were commonly held in Sokol halls. The importance of establishing Sokol units was demonstrated by the immigrant's, willingness to donate money, participate in fund drives, and volunteer their time and labor. The development of gymnastic programs, mainly in the cities, was aided by

Some earlier Sokol halls were constructed from wood. Top figure is Brush Creek, Nebraska Sokol hall built in 1888 (photo is circa 1920). Photos at bottom are Budivoj Sokol in Detroit, circa late 19th century (left) and Czech-Havlíček in Cleveland, circa early 20th century (right).

hiring competent trainers from the Czech lands, who welcomed the opportunities available in the New World. The enthusiastic immigrants also developed Sokol programs in small towns that had adequate numbers of Czechs. For example: by 1908, there were fifteen Sokol units in Nebraska of which thirteen were in small towns. Sokol halls, in the cities, usually had libraries, consistent with the goal of a "sound mind in a sound body." Their holdings were not limited to gymnastics and fitness topics, but also included books on Czech culture and history. As the various units grew, they often developed summer camps which provided activities and opportunities for children and teenagers to interact with nature.

Sokol Training for Women

Gymnastic training for women in Sokol occurred in America before it did in the Czech lands, because women's rights were not resisted as fervently as in the Austrian and Austro-Hungarian Empires, where women were forbidden to wear Sokol uniforms or march in parades. St. Louis had a women's auxiliary *(Dámský Odbor Sokola Vlasta)* as early as 1876, whose main purpose was raising money for the men's group, and participating in theater and education. After 1878, women's groups began developing in other Sokol units, such as the one in New York City, where the creation of a girl's division evolved into the Gymnastic Club for Ladies and Girls. During the 1890s women's groups grew, and in 1893 women's membership was considered on an equal basis with men, but women did not serve in leadership roles.

At the national convention in 1903, the delegates voted to establish women's units and auxiliaries, and a year later, at the National Unity Sokol Slet in St. Louis, women competed for the first time. An important decision by the American Sokol Organization Executive Committee in 1921 was that women take over leadership roles for all female gymnastic activities. This change was in response to Mildred Prchal's request, a Sokol leader who played a major role as an advocate for women's artistic and later rhythmic gymnastics. A Women's Board of Instructors at the unit and district levels was approved a year later, and in 1923 the first combined Instructor's School for women and men was conducted. Today women outnumber men in Sokol gymnastic participation.

Unification of Sokol Units in America

National Unity Sokol (NUS)

A call for unification. The sixteen Sokol units in existence in 1878 (Table 3) each interpreted the Tyrš system of gymnastics independently. To rectify this problem, Sokol New York proposed that all units should work together in order to uniformly utilize the system according to one set of rules and bylaws (Barcal, 1990). This call for unity led to the formation, in 1878, of the first national Sokol organization, the *Národní Jednota Sokolská* (NJS) or National Unity Sokol (NUS). Ten units joined at that time: two units from Chicago (Gymnastic Unit Sokol in Chicago, and Sokol Czech-American), two from Cedar Rapids (Sokol Tyrš Cedar Rapids and Sokol Club Cedar Rapids), and one each from New York, Baltimore (Blesk), St Louis, Cleveland, Detroit, and Kewaunee, Wisconsin. A year later the first national competitions were held in New York, and NUS began publishing *Sokol Americký* (American Sokol), which still exists today. This first national competition included only nineteen men from seven units, and NUS underwent growing pains for several decades (reviewed by Nolte, 2011, 79–80). After the 1879 gymnastics competition, the next three competitions, between 1881 and 1887, included fewer than fifty men, but finally in 1891, 123 men participated. These early NUS competitions lacked the displays of mass calisthenics, characteristic of Slets, but are listed along with the subsequent Slets (Table 4).

Obstacles to unification. One of the obstacles for the growth of NUS was the failure of many units to join the national organization, some because they did not want to pay extra fees, and others because of the competition between Chicago and New York for leadership in NUS, or differences of whether insurance programs should be offered by the organization (Nolte, 2011, 80). Another issue arose in some Chicago units that objected to the use of English in training sessions, which led to the formation of *Župa Fügner-Tyrš* (District Fuegner-Tyrš) in 1897, an organization that consisted of ten units by 1905. They were called "red" Sokols because they wore the elaborate uniform of the Czech Sokols that included a bright red Garibaldi shirt. In contrast, NUS members were called "blues" due to their choice of uniforms. The two organizations did not collaborate until 1913. *Dělnický Americký* (D.A.) Sokol (American Worker's Sokol), founded in 1892, was yet another Czech-American Sokol organization.

NUS had a five-point plan of purpose (Nolte, 2011, 77–8). During the first meeting of the NUS, the purpose of the organization was stated in a plan with five objectives as summerized here:

1. Mutual support of members in training men healthy in body and spirit.
2. Support our nationality by a) founding gymnastic units and schools, and b) founding libraries for educational, gymnastic, and entertainment uses.
3. Recognition of education and morality as the only roads to the reform of social, political, and religious life.
4. Oppose any elimination of personal freedom and rights, because they go against the development and growth of our free system.
5. Provide mutual insurance in the case of death.

Growth of National Union Sokol Units. The inaugural meeting of the organization addressed a controversial issue, namely a standard Sokol uniform. The military-style uniform of the Czech Sokols was considered too flamboyant, thus NUS selected a blue suit and white shirt with a Sokol symbol on the belt buckle. The impressive growth of Sokol units corresponded, at least in part, to the increasing numbers of Czech immigrants during the last decade of the 19th century and the first decade of the 20th century. In 1894, NUS included thirty-five units (See Appendix A) with about 1,000 members, but by 1909 there were sixty-seven units with more than 5,000 members (Nolte, 2011, 78). In 1908, Chicago had the largest representation of any city, whereas, Nebraska had the most units of any state. Appendix B lists the units and districts comprising NUS in 1917.

Sokol Free Thinkers. "Free thought" was a philosophy of most Czech Sokol members under Austrian rule and was consistent with their hopes for nationhood (Nešpor, 2004, 282–284). Free thinkers were especially skeptical of religious dogma which was fueled by the Austrian Government's support of Roman Catholic clerics who insisted on social superiority, privileges, and blind acceptance of clerical direc-

tives. Thus, anti-clericalism was common among Sokol members. Aware of the oppressive conditions under the Habsburg rule, the American immigrants were conscious of parochial influences, and therefore emphasized "free-thinking" a term that became a hallmark of the organization. Radical free thinkers in NUS asserted that it was the obligation of Sokols to deliver its members from the influence of other "worldly religious, so-called, education" (Nolte, 2011, 82). Looking back at the original intentions of the Sokol philosophy, this imposition of controlling a member's religious beliefs clearly violated the very concept of "free thinking." In 1893, NUS issued a statement of its purpose which stated, "to undertake the spiritual and physical development of young people, women and men, and work for progress and the cultivation of our people in this land according to the principles of citizenship and of Free Thought." Statements such as this limited the organization's goal of spiritual and physical growth by its narrow definition of "free thinking." Indeed, the idea of free thinking was exclusive rather than inclusive. Alienated, a Czech-American minority formed the Catholic Sokol in the 1890s, an organization that consisted of very few units. Another political liability of the early NUS was its conciliatory posture toward socialism, which related to free thought, and the labor movement. In contrast, the *ČOS* avoided any obvious political stances in their organization because of the Habsburg authorities.

The Sokol mission in America. With the formation of NUS, the entire system of gymnastics utilized by the Czechs in Prague was mandated. Moreover, the idea that the educational mission is not an independent goal, but rather an integral part of the Tyrš gymnastic system was affirmed. This issue had been raised in Prague by a *ČOS* member who was an advocate for a separate department of education within the organization that would be on par with gymnastics. Such a suggestion was fraught with political baggage and was promptly rejected. As noted by Karel Prchal (1949), the endeavors on which Sokol was founded, i.e., "call for healthy bodies and souls, (therefore) we strive to improve our members physically, mentally, and spiritually." These goals are not separate understandings, but rather are expressed in unity. Sokol was established as a system of gymnastics and was recognized as such by the founders of the Sokol units in the United States. The importance of participation in the fitness program, as highlighted in the 1883 NUS by-laws, included the requirement that all Sokol members under the age of twenty-five must attend gymnastics classes.

Chicago's 1893 World Fair (Columbia Exposition). A Sokol Slet (officially number VI) was held in conjunction with this event and included NUS and other Sokol organizations. The opening day, designated as "Czech Day," featured a parade, concert, and Sokol exhibition. A highlight of the festivities was a concert directed by the beloved Czech composer, Antonin Dvořák. The parade assembled near *Plzeňský* (Pilsen) Sokol Hall on Ashland Avenue included about 20,000 participants who marched to the sounds of large cheering crowds (Smith, 2019). Gymnastic participants included 360 men, 275 women, and 368 children performing mass calisthenics and 194 men competing in gymnastics (Table 4). The gymnastic exhibits, held in a 15,000-capacity arena included a grand finale of teams of men demonstrating their skill on every piece of apparatus. *ČOS* members who participated were impressed with the fact that many Sokol units were being established in the US, and presented NUS with a letter of appreciation and a silver wreath of Slavonic linden leaves in honor of their Czech countrymen in America. The letter noted the zealous work of Sokols in America. This was the first time that NUS fielded an impressive number of gymnasts performing mass exercises characteristic of Slets. The one-week long event was described in the *National Heritage Chronicles* as "the most magnificent demonstration of National awareness of a Czech Colony in America."

NUS forms districts. A power struggle between Czech Sokols in New York and Chicago developed because each group wanted the national office in their city (Jožák, 1998, 58). Debates concerning the issue persisted during the next three years. Because two sets of officers were elected in 1888, NUS had headquarters in both New York and Chicago; during the next six years Milwaukee hosted the national headquarters. In 1894, New York became NUS headquarters until 1914 when it was relocated in Chicago, where it remained. As reported by Barcal (1990, 4–11), in 1894, the thirty-five Sokol units were assigned to one of four districts: Eastern (New York), Central (Milwaukee), Chicago, and Western (Omaha). As seen in Appendix A, eight of the units were in very small towns

(six in Nebraska and one each in Iowa and Illinois). This fact reveals the determination of Czech immigrants to form Sokol units wherever they settled, even in small, farm communities. However, of these eight units only Nebraska's Crete and Wilber Sokols exist today. The number of districts was increased from four to six in 1910 with the addition of the Southern and Pacific Districts to accommodate sixty-five units (Barcal, 1990, 8–9). The increase in the number of NUS units is seen by comparing Appendix B to Appendix A.

Training instructors. Already at the 1888 convention, held in Omaha, the delegates voted to conduct schools for instructors on a national level, which corresponded to the model of the Czech Sokols. This was essential for the development of competent instructors and uniform teaching of the Tyrš system. These instructor schools (courses) still exist and are usually held during the summer.

National Unity Sokol Slets. The success of the Sokol display during the 1893 Chicago World's Fair drew attention to the Sokol movement and was followed by four more NUS Slets (Table 4): 1900 in Cleveland, 1904 in St. Louis, 1909 in Chicago, and 1914 in Omaha. Women competed in NUS Slets beginning in 1904, but only in calisthenics. The VI to X Slets included a few hundred competitors and 700 to 1400 men, women, juniors, and children performing calisthenics (Barcal, 1990, 7–14). Following World War I, the American Sokol Organization was formed and continues as the national organization for Czech-American Sokols.

NUS, Zupa Fügner-Tyrš and Dělnický Americký (D.A.) Sokols consider a merger. A desire to coordinate all Sokol gymnastic and technical activities under a common leadership was recognized as a means of promoting the Tyrš system. This goal was considered by a committee of the three Sokol organizations in 1917. Although all other Sokol societies, e.g., Slovak Gymnastic Union Sokol, Slovak Catholic Sokol, were invited to merge with them, they decided to continue their independence. The merger of the three societies occurred and the American Sokol Organization (ASO) became the national governing body in 1917. However, in 1919, D.A. Sokols withdrew from ASO, and have remained independent. By 1933 eight districts formed the ASO (Appendix C). For a listing of the various units existing in 1961, 1994, and 2008 see Appendices D, E, and F.

American Sokol Organization (ASO)

The road to unification. During the first decade of the 20th century, the need to merge Sokol organizations began to be realized. As common goals became more obvious, both NUS and District Fügner-Tyrš Sokols took part in some of the same celebrations. One such event was a "Sokol Day" celebration in Chicago in 1905, an event that also included the Slovak and Croatian Sokols, as well as ČOS (Czech Organization Sokol). Then in 1909 the Czech championship team took part in the NUS Slet in Chicago, which also included participation of the District Fügner-Tyrš Sokols. This event helped negate some of the old prejudices. Thus, a sense of brotherhood began to take hold. This new openness and the recognition of common goals paved the road for the initial integration of the three Sokol societies, as noted above, under a single banner, the ASO. The first Slet of the new ASO in 1921, held in Chicago, included 1,350 men, women, juniors, and boys and girls who performed mass calisthenics (Table 5). Competitions on apparatus were limited to men, whereas women competed in calisthenics only. In 1923, ASO had 10,000 members (Chada, 1981, 143), and by 1926 membership had increased to 12,611 (Barcal, 1990, 27). In 1944, despite the occurrence of World War II, ASO still had 106 units in seven districts and 10,000 members (Jelinek and Zmrhal, 1944). Appendices C, D, E, and F list the ASO units and districts for the years 1933, 1961, 1994, and 2008.

Gymnastic instructors from Czechoslovakia. The 1921 Slet hosted the men's Czechoslovak Sokol gymnastic team, who then toured the USA and inspired American gymnasts. Three of the team's members later played key roles as instructors in ASO units. Jarka Jelinek, who became a legendary American Sokol, served as National Men's Director. Frank Machovsky and Stanley Matoska became instructors at Cedar Rapids, Iowa, and Berwyn, Illinois, Sokols, respectively. It was immigrants such as these highly trained gymnasts and teachers that brought the Sokol movement in America to a higher level. Subsequently, others made the voyage to America and brought with them a wealth of knowledge regarding gymnastics, as well as the philosophy and implementation of the Sokol system. One such immigrant, who came in 1948, was Marie Provazníková, who played a major role in both gymnastics and physical education, as a teacher, organizer, and coach. Her contributions are noted in Chapters 2 and 5.

Charles (Karel) Prchal (1896–1980), a lifetime of leadership. A Czech immigrant, who became an architect, is remembered for his devotion to the Sokol movement. He was a member of Sokol Havlíček-Tyrš and later Sokol Tabor in Berwyn, and served as American Sokol Organization President for thirty-one years. His numerous publications provided a cornerstone for Sokol's mission and its role in Czech and Czech-American history. Prchal traveled to virtually every Sokol unit with his message of encouragement and support, and has been honored by many national and international organizations for his contributions. Because he was highly respected, Prchal was very effective in promoting the interests of Sokol. He was married to Mildred Prchal, the legendary leader of gymnastic programs and an inductee of US Gymnastics Hall of Fame (see Chapter 5). Together this couple provided the most important Sokol leadership in the 20th century.

Zupa (District) Fügner-Tyrš

When established in 1897, this organization consisted of six Sokol units—Sokol Slávský (men), Sokolice Slávský (women), Sokol Pokrok, Sokol Zisku Dub, Sokolice Zisku Dub, Sokol Slavia—all of which were in the Chicago area (Barcal, 1990). Zupa Fügner-Tyrš shared the values and programs of National Union Sokol except for the uniform, which, as noted earlier, included the red shirt, and was the source of the organization's nick name "Red Sokols." One other difference was the insistence on the use of the Czech language in their gym classes. Zupa Fügner-Tyrš organized six Slets during its nineteen years of existence, and limited competition to men. When the organization merged with NUS and D.A. Sokol, it had twenty-four units in the US and one in Frank, Alberta Canada. Thirteen of the units were in the Chicago area, with five women's units included in this number. Six units were in Ohio and three were in Wisconsin.

Dělnické Americký (D.A.) Sokol

Czech immigrants in America recalled the class division between the working men and the noblemen in their Habsburg-controlled fatherland. These memories precipitated discussions of an organization that would bring together the working class, and led to the formation of a workers (dělnické) group. Their familiarity and cultural identification with the Tyrš system led them to form a Sokol organization. Thus, on March 14, 1892, 46 men met in Manhattan and formed an organization named Dělnické Americký (D.A.) Sokol. That first meeting was under the leadership of Gustav Haberman, who later became the first Minister of Education and Affairs of the Czechoslovak Republic. The anthropologist, Dr. Aleš Hrdlick was his assistant, and later became Curator in the Smithsonian Institutes Division of Physical Anthropology. By September of 1892, a Women's Division was founded. A quarterly journal of the organization, Beseda Sokolska, first appeared in 1894. Before the turn of the century, other units were established in the New York City area, and a D.A. Sokol Hall was erected there in 1908.

The organization's philosophy was that promoted by Miroslav Tyrš, and shared with other Sokol organizations, i.e., "a sound body in a sound mind." Between 1892 and 1915, fifteen men's and nine women's units were established. Most were in or close to the New York City metropolitan area. However, a joint association with a D.A. Sokol unit in Cleveland, in 1934, enabled joint exhibitions and instructor's courses in Cleveland's Camp Taborville. In the early 20th century, D.A. Sokol men participated in various gymnastic competitions, and in 1914 D.A. Sokol became a member of New York Metropolitan Amateur Athletic Union. In 1927, and again in 1934, D.A. Sokol men's and women's teams participated in competitions in Prague. In 1939, a "Czechoslovakia Day" was organized by the Joint Councils of Czechoslovak Societies of the New York area in conjunction with all Sokol units in the area. The celebration was held in New York City's Triboro Stadium and was considered an outstanding show of unity between the various Czech organizations. D.A. Sokol and the Slovak Gymnastic Union Sokol, along with Sokol teams from Czechoslovakia, sponsored an Olympiad at the Triboro Stadium in 1947. A regularly scheduled school for gymnastics instructors was developed in the early 1950s. Frank Safanda, a member of the New York City D. A. Sokol, was a member of the 1924 US Olympic gymnastics team.

Worker's Gymnastic Union (Dělnicka Tělocvična Jednota)

A group of Czech immigrants in Cleveland founded this organization, like the D.A. Sokols, in 1909, which like its counterpart in Bohemia was aimed at promoting democracy and gymnastics among laborers. At its peak, there were 16 clubs in the US, but currently only one unit (Taborville, Ohio) is active.

Catholic Union Sokol

The first Catholic Sokol club was organized in Omaha in 1893, as an affiliate of St. Wenceslaus parish in the heart of "Little Bohemia," Omaha's first Czech settlement (Kucera, 1976, 211–212). Many other lodges were then formed: first in South Omaha and then in six small towns in Nebraska, as well in cities, e.g., Chicago, Baltimore, and Detroit. In response to a call for an organization of the various groups, Katolický (Catholic) Sokol, a national organization was founded in 1908, and during the second decade of the 20th century included seventy clubs (Chada, 1981, 143–144). The clubs were usually associated or affiliated with a parish, like those in Omaha and Chicago, and in 1909, some of the clubs participated in the Chicago Slet. A few were able to own their own buildings. Gymnastic exhibitions were held by many of the clubs, and they participated in district meets. A major goal of the Catholic Union Sokol was to cultivate a double standard of patriotism, i.e., first for the United States and then for Bohemia. The organization did not flourish after World War I.

Orel

An Orel (Eagle) movement originated in 1902 in Moravia in response to the Czech Sokol Organization's barring religious events in Sokol Club ceremonies (Nolte, 2002, 154). Nevertheless, Orel members wore Sokol uniforms and protested a moral decline in the Sokol Organization and had a few clubs in the US.

Sokol Canada

Prior to 1911, there were no Czech or Slovak societies in Canada, but that year Czech immigrants established a Sokol club in Michel, British Columbia, and another in nearby Frank, Alberta, towns in Western Canada's coal mining region. These units were the first Czech ethnic clubs in Canada. However, coal mining decreased during the decade, and in 1917 the mines were closed. The loss of employment opportunities caused the two units to lose members, which resulted in their closing in the early 1930s. All other units in Canada were formed after World War I: Winnipeg (1927), Montreal (1928), Toronto (1931), and Regina (1932). These units experienced the consequences of separation from each other by great distances. Thus, their interactions were limited. Sokol in Batawa, Ontario, was established in 1940, whereas, all other units in Canada were founded, during a twenty-nine-year period, after World War II. In 1950, a second unit was established in Montreal (Masaryk- Montreal), followed by six more: Kitchener, Ontario (1952), Windsor, Ontario, and a second unit in Toronto (1953), Noranda, Quebec (1955), Ottawa (1962), and Vancouver (1969). Sokol Batawa came into existence with the development of the town by Czech and Slovak immigrants, who had recently immigrated and found employment in the Bata Shoe Company of Zlin, Czechoslovakia. The proximity of Batawa to Toronto facilitated joint activities with the unit in Toronto, as well as interactions with ASO units in Cleveland, Detroit, and Toledo.

When the Communist government was formed in 1948 in Czechoslovakia, many Czechs and Slovaks settled in Canada. Twenty years later another surge of immigrants settled in Canada in 1968 in response to the Soviet-lead invasion of their country. These new settlers contributed significantly to an increase to Sokol activities. A national organization (Sokol Canada) was established in 1952, which enabled an increase in contacts and interactions with Sokols on an international scale. Consequently, national Slets and an annual Canadian National Gymnastics Championships became traditional events. Sokol Canada sponsors summer activities, which include competitions in track and field, and swimming, as well as camping in Canada's Laurentian Mountains (north of Montreal). During the winter months skiing and skating competitions are held. Sokols in Canada have been leaders in the development of gymnastics in their country by organizing, officiating and competing in meets. They have also organized teams for other sports, e.g., volleyball and weightlifting, and have contributed to the Canadian Government's National Advisory Council on Fitness and Amateur Sport.

Sokols Founded by Slovak and Polish Immigrants

These two groups of immigrants founded Sokol units in the US like those established by the Czechs. Although Slovaks and Poles are Slavs, as are Czechs, and their Sokol organizations were like those of the Czechs, their ethnic histories differ. Slovaks, who were under Hungarian rule, were "not considered an individual people, but merely Slovaks speaking Hungarian" (*The Slovak Catholic Story*, 2005, 50). Unlike the Czechs, the Slovaks were not able to develop a Sokol movement on their behalf in Hungary. The establishment of Slovak Sokols began first in the 1890s in the US, rather than in Hungarian Slovakia; formation of their clubs on the East Coast was facilitated by the Czech-American Sokols, as the Slovaks adapted the Tyrš system and became closely aligned with the NUS and later ASO. Polish Falcons originated in their homeland and utilized the gymnastic systems of Sokols and the German Turners. Although the Poles were mostly under Russian rule, they maintained a sense of national unity and formed some political movements. Thus, though not identical, the struggles of the Czechs, Slovaks, and Poles were similar in that they sought freedom and national identity.

Sokol USA (Slovak Gymnastic Union Sokol)

Origin and fraternal benefits. Like the Czech immigrants, Slovak immigrants in their US communities formed Sokol clubs, which they called lodges. It is not surprising that the first Slovak Sokols were established nearly three decades after the first Czech-American Sokol in St. Louis. Because Sokol in Slovakia under the Hungarian Empire was not permitted, Slovaks did not experience the Sokol movement so familiar to Czechs under Habsburg's rule in Bohemia and Moravia. Nevertheless, Slovak immigrants, mostly those who arrived in the 1890s took to the idea of the Sokol movement. A few months after the first lodge was established in Chicago in 1892, the Slovak National-Cultural Society ("Slavia") in New York was renamed Slovak Sokol of New York, and then in 1895 the "Young Men's Slovak Society" was established in Bridgeport, Connecticut. The Czech immigrants rallied to the Slovak's desire to establish Sokol clubs, especially in New York. Despite having only a few lodges, the Slovak Gymnastic Union Sokol (SGUS) was formed on July 4, 1896, and two years later the Women's Slovak Sokol Organization was founded. The women's organization merged with SGUS in 1912. SGUS was founded as a nonsectarian fraternal benefit society that provides insurance, as well as gymnastic and social programs. The role of SGUS as a benevolent society was initially problematic, but later was recognized as a strength of the organization. SGUS held its first convention in 1898, and by 1905 there were ninety men's lodges with 2,500 members in eight states: New York, New Jersey, Connecticut, Massachusetts, Pennsylvania, Ohio, Illinois, and Wisconsin. That year the first issue of *Slovenský Sokol,* later renamed *Sokol Times,* the society's official journal was published. Consistent with the fact that most Slovaks settled in the eastern and northeastern sections of the US, SGUS lodges were not formed west of the Mississippi.

Slets. The first SGUS Slet was held in 1906 with 223 gymnasts representing twelve lodges, and in 1907 SGUS gymnasts participated in the All-Sokol Slet in Prague. During the first three decades of the 20th century, SGUS grew as indicated by the increase in the number of districts from six to twelve, the building of approximately fifteen halls with gymnasiums, and the development of an extensive training literature. In 1910, there were 210 lodges with 5,826 members; three Slets were held between 1906 and 1913 (Josak, 1998, 77). By 1920, the organization consisted of 237 adult lodges with 8,219 members, as well as eighty-six juvenile branches. In 1922, independent Slovak Sokol units joined SGUS, and in 1925, the American Sokol Organization and SGUS joined in the 1925 Slet, held in Chicago's Soldier Field with 3,478 gymnasts participating in front of 40,000 spectators. Thereafter, SGUS and ASO members continued participating in each other's Slets.

Membership. In 1935, SGUS had 12,359 adult and 7,195 juvenile members, however, not all the lodges offered gymnastics training, and thus were limited to the insurance offerings of the organization. New activities were introduced in the mid-20th century: Annual SGUS National Bowling Tournament (1948), and Annual SGUS National Golf tournament (1950). SGUS officially became Sokol USA in 1962. A sharp decline in Sokol USA membership occurred during the last three decades of the 20th century, paralleling that of the American Sokol Organization. Thus, in the year

2,000 there were eighty-two lodges, but only eleven that offered gymnastic training (Slavik, 2000, 438–439).

Slovak Catholic Sokol

Roots of the organization. Most Slovak immigrants were Christian, primarily Catholic or Lutheran, and they organized parishes in their communities. The Sokol movement, dominated by Free Thinkers, was generally hostel to religion. Because the Slovak Gymnastic Union Sokol often held activities on Sunday mornings, this practice conflicted with participation in Sunday church services. Some members feared the secular and anti-Catholic programs with the parent organization (Tanzone, 2005, 22–53). To resolve this issue, a group of Slovak immigrants from Passaic, New Jersey, petitioned to have a lodge for those of the Catholic faith, thereby enabling their members full participation in the Sokol traditions, while remaining active in their church. The parent organization denied the petition of the Passaic group. This rejection was based, in part, by the desire of the Passaic group to have a lodge exclusively for Catholics. The result of this decision led to the formation, in 1905, of the Roman and Greek Catholic Gymnastic Union Sokol; during the 1933 convention, the name was shortened to Slovak Catholic Sokol and death benefits for spouses were included for members. Passaic, New Jersey, became the organization's headquarters and delegates chose the motto: *Za Boha a Narod (For God and Country).* An overview of the organization's history is provided by Tanzone (1995 and 2005).

Organization's dual role. Slovak Catholic Sokol is an Athletic Fraternal Benefits Society, and in addition to its athletic and fraternal missions, has a role in benevolence that includes grants for students (elementary, high school, and college). The organization's clubs are called "assemblies" and during earlier times women had separate clubs that were called "wreaths." Membership was open to women by 1908, and by 1910, just five years after the organization was established, there were forty-four assemblies and eighteen wreaths, with a combined membership of 1,800. In 1926, Slovak Catholic Sokol membership had grown five-fold to 9,172, and that year members of the organization participated in the 1926 Slet in Prague. By 1950, membership reached 39,000 and assets exceeded one million dollars. The financial solvency is a key to the organization's survival. The Slovak Catholic Sokol organization holds Slets every two years and clinics prior to each Slet.

Polish Falcons of America

Polish gymnastic clubs, based on the Sokol movement and the German Turnvereins, were first established in Poland in 1867, and then in 1887, the first Polish Falcon lodge (called "nest") was formed in Chicago, a city that already had a large Polish population. Other Polish communities also formed Polish Falcon nests, so that by 1894 there were a total of twelve, which led to the formation of a charter: Alliance of Polish Turners of the United States of America. The organization merged with the Polish National Alliance (PNA). A dissident group called the "Free Falcons" was formed in 1909, but they united with PNA. The early success of the Czech Sokol movement resulted in the availability of enough gymnastics teachers, which, due to the close ties between Czechs and Poles, provided the Polish Falcon groups with both instructors and the use of Sokol facilities (Pienkos, 1987, 20–21). Since 1928, the Polish Falcons of America have operated a fraternal insurance association. The Polish National Alliance's first constitution in 1894 "opened its membership to all Poles above the age of eighteen who were found to be of good moral character according to the precepts of the Roman Catholic Church" (Pienkos, 1987, 39–40). This is not surprising because most Polish immigrants were Roman Catholics and did not bring with them the anticlerical sentiments so prevalent in the Czech Sokol movement.

During World War I, the Falcons participated in Officer's Training Schools in the USA and Canada and later served in the Polish Army, and in 1917, when the USA entered the war, many joined the US Army (Kuzma, 2000). At the onset of the 21st century, there were 29,000 Falcon members and 100 nests. The primary focus of Polish Falcons was like that of Czech and Slovak organizations after World War I: gymnastics, mass calisthenics, group fitness training, and track and field events. Over the years many other sports have been added to the Polish Falcons list of activities, e.g., softball, golf, and bowling. Biannual competitions in various sports, called "Zlots," are held in many districts and a National Zlot is held every four years to coincide with the national conventions.

Sokol Commemorative Stamp

In 1960, the American Sokol Organization (ASO) Convention in Cedar Rapids urged its Executive Board to "secure the issuance of a commemorative stamp honoring the upcoming centennial of the Sokol Movement in America" (Cermak, 1966, 31–32). At the invitation of the ASO, other Sokol organizations joined this effort, and on November 20, 1963, a formal memorandum for a stamp honoring Sokol was presented to Postmaster General John Gronouski. Support for this request was beyond expectations, as many letters from cultural, fraternal, and professional organizations, and from thousands of Sokol members were submitted. Of special importance were the testimonies of children regarding the value of Sokol training in their lives. Consequently, the Sokol's training of thousands of Americans was recognized, and the Sokol Physical Fitness Stamp was issued on February 15, 1965.

Summary/Conclusions

Czech immigrants had much the same vision as other ethnic groups, i.e., freedom and opportunity. However, because 97% of Czech immigrants were literate and many were skilled, they had an advantage over most other ethnic groups. Settlements were established in small rural communities as well as in cities, and were characterized by a Czech culture which included the formation of Sokol clubs (units). Sokol provided not only physical training, but also a community center for various cultural groups, e.g., drama, choral, and dance. Sokol units also often provided libraries, lectures, Czech classes, and social functions. Czech immigrants contributed to American life in many ways: journalism, literature, politics, and education. Just three years after the formation of the first Sokol in Prague, a Sokol unit was established in St. Louis, and seven more were founded between 1866 and 1870. Unification of the Sokol units began in 1878 with the formation of National Unity Sokol (NUS), which provided a uniformity of interpretation of the Tyrš system, as more units were established and assembled into districts. Finally, in 1917, a more complete alignment of the 121 units occurred when the American Sokol Organization became the governing body. Sokol in the US is an immigrant story that provided one of the most important links to Czech culture. As these Czech settlers assimilated, they maintained their culture, thus Sokol was preserved through successive generations.

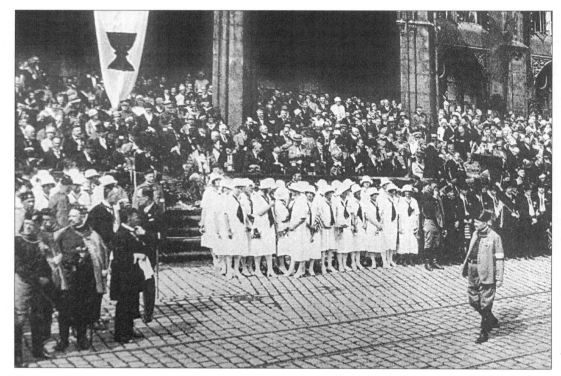

Women representing the American Sokol Organization, dressed in white uniforms, are seen watching the 1926 Sokol Slet parade in Prague.

American Sokol Organization Slet held in 1925 in Soldier Field (Chicago), with over 400 women performing calisthenics. Photo from American Sokol Organization

Sokol gymnasts in the US.
Top left: Courtesy of *Omaha World Herald*
Bottom right: Courtesy of *The Gazette* (Eastern Iowa)

4

Establishing Sokol Units in Czech Settlements

Introduction

During the late 19th and early 20th centuries, as Czech settlements were established in both small towns and large cities, Sokol clubs were formed. These clubs, as previously noted, were called units, and were most often a magnet for Czech cultural activities, including theater, vocal and dance groups, lectures, and fraternal groups. The purpose of this chapter is to provide some insights into how these units were formed and grew, and their unique contributions to their communities and members. The histories of all Czech Sokol units in America is beyond the scope of this book. Data listing the Sokol units belonging to the National Unity Sokol and then to the American Sokol Organization are found in Appendices A–E. Some Sokol Gyms consisted of two or more, rarely three, "units," because women and men had separate jurisdictions (each had their own officers and boards). However, they used the same facilities and most often shared the same instructors.

The Earliest Sokol Units (1865–1875)

St. Louis, Chicago, and New York

Sokol St. Louis. The first Sokol unit in the US was launched from a meeting on February 14, 1865, under the direction of three founders: J.B. Erben, Karel Procháska and Jaroslav Vostrovský. The formation of this first unit was discussed in Chapter 3, but it is well to note that it endured many struggles during its first three decades. It lost critical leadership when Karel Procháska, and Jaroslav Vostrovský moved away a year after St. Louis Sokol was established. Moreover, there existed problems with the buildings being utilized, which caused cancellations of gymnastic activities. Subsequently, the unit held their classes at the German

Turner Hall, but after the instructor left, classes were again cancelled. However, in 1875 Sokol St. Louis was reorganized and finally in 1890 joined the new Bohemian National Hall as shareholders. Because the building's gymnasium facilities were inadequate, the Sokols purchased Union Capital Hall. The new Sokol home was a center for many groups and activities, in addition to gymnastics, other activities included choral and instrumental music groups, Czech plays, balls, and dances. In 1896, a storm damaged the hall, but activities continued and in 1922 Sokol St. Louis moved into the new National Hall, located in a Czech neighborhood; they became co-owners and major shareholders of the building. The unit thrived in the new National Hall. A year later, they purchased land in a rural area, and over the years a summer camp, with a large lodge, and a swimming pool was developed. The stability of the unit was largely due to a qualified gymnastic instructor since 1894, and then the continuing service of a Czech-born gymnastics champion and instructor, Frank Prihoda, who arrived in the mid-1930s, and served until 1965.

Gymnastic Unit Sokol (Tělocvičná Jednota Sokol) in Chicago. On August 19, 1866, the second Sokol unit in the US, and the first in Chicago, was organized with 59 charter members. Two years later the unit merged with *Slovanská Lípa* (Slavic Linden), a Czech cultural organization that provided space in their building for gymnastic training. In 1871, the unit adopted the name "Gymnastic Unit Sokol of Chicago" and became owners of the building, which was located on Clinton Street near Van Buren. Because many Czechs began settling in new subdivisions, such as "New Tabor," a new unit, Sokol Tabor was organized in 1890, however their building was destroyed by fire two years later. Then in 1914, Sokol Tabor merged with *Sokol Slovanská Lípa* and the new unit became Sokol Tabor-Slavic Linden (using the English version for the name).

Sokol New York. Many Czech youths belonged to a club called *"Včela"* (Bee) and were inspired by the German Turnverein in their city. Based on the news they received about Sokols in Bohemia and Moravia, they were encouraged that a Sokol Unit could exist in New York City. The young men brought the idea to meetings of *Včela,* and on October 13, 1867, *Včela* became Gymnastic Unit Sokol New York, consisting of 60 members. Just a year later *Slovanská Lípa, Hlahol* (a choral group), and Sokol united and formed four departments: gymnastics, singing, drama, and education. They also published a weekly newspaper. Because the union soon dispersed, Sokol training was conducted in various locations in the city. However, enthusiasm for Sokol gymnastics grew, and in 1894 land was purchased on East 71st Street in Manhattan. Each member was required to contribute $50, within four years, for the erection of a Sokol Hall, and on July 12, 1896, the cornerstone of the Bohemian Gymnastic Association Sokol Hall in New York was laid. The dedication event drew praise from the *New York Times,* which applauded the event as a "holiday for Bohemians," and noted the contributions of Bohemians in the city, and that the unit at that time had 495 members. The building continues to stand as a practical and impressive facility. Each interest group of the unit had a board to promote and oversee its activities. These groups included Drama, Choral, Friends and Wives of Sokol, and Children's and Women's Bugle and Drum. Sokol New York has thrived for more than 150 years because it has maintained its programs, has paid instructors, a large membership, and an ideal location. The success of Sokol New York can be attributed to many factors, e.g., location, facilities, and a variety of programs. The unit offers both artistic and rhythmic gymnastics, Tae Kwon Do, modern dance, ballet, senior fitness, volleyball and basketball. Sokol New York has maintained historical documents of the unit, and its library has more than three thousand titles.

Sokol New York was a vibrant unit, even during its earliest decades, as detailed in their Golden Jubilee Commemoration *(Památník T.J. Sokol v New Yorku, 1917).* Their gymnasts were very active in competitive gymnastics, winning numerous awards in both Sokol and non-Sokol competitions. In 1909, Frank Jirasek distinguished himself as the best US all-around gymnast and in 1910 the Sokol New York team won the National AAU championship. Subsequently, two of its members earned spots on US Olympic teams, and four were inducted into the US Gymnastics Hall of Fame (see Chapter 5 for details).

Sokol Svornost, Morrisania, New York. The borough of the Bronx includes the section called Morrisania, which was a Czech settlement, where Sokol Svornost was founded in 1867, the same year that Sokol New York was established. Morrisania was rural in the late 19th century and was favored as a vacation spot by Manhattan Bohemians. Sokol Svornost had ties with Sokol Kutna Hora in Bohemia. The unit utilized the German Turner gym for their classes and established a library in 1872. A major problem for the unit was that growth in membership was clearly inadequate *(Památník Sokola Pražskeho,* 1883, 290–1). In 1883, there were only sixteen members, and only an average of six to seven members attended meetings.

Other Early Czech Sokol Units

Sokol Milwaukee. Bohemian and Moravian immigrants were among the first ethnic groups to settle in Milwaukee and other Wisconsin towns. A group of Milwaukee Czechs met on June 14, 1868, in the upstairs meeting room of the Meister Brewery, and there formed the fifth Sokol Unit in the US (the Milwaukee Sokol Gymnastic Union). In 1869, the group merged with *Slovanská Lípa,* a merger that also occurred with other Sokols, as noted previously. Four years after Sokol Milwaukee was founded, the organization established a Czech school, and in 1873 a new facility was built, in order to accommodate the many new immigrant members who settled in the city. Theatrical and choral groups were established and affiliated with the Sokol unit. Then in 1879, Sokol Milwaukee merged with CSPS (Czech-Slovak Protective Society), but the merger did not agree with some members, who then, a year later formed *Věrní Bratří* (Loyal Brothers) Sokol. This new Sokol unit lasted only a decade. Two important events in the 1890s were: 1) formation of the Ladies and Girl's Gymnastic Society, and 2) the construction of *Česko-americká síň* (Czech-American Hall), which opened in 1895. The building came to be known as the "Bohemian Hall," a structure that contained a gymnasium, theater, classrooms, and meeting rooms. It was the combined efforts of Sokol Milwaukee, CSPS, and Lodges Wisconsin and *Čechoslovan* that Bohemian Hall was erected. Sokol Milwaukee enjoyed good relations with the German Turners and held annual gymnastics competitions with them.

Sokol Blesk, Baltimore. The many Czechs employed in a cigar factory in this East Coast city discussed the need to establish a Sokol unit, which led to the founding of *Sokolská Jednota* (sokol unit) Blesk in 1872 with sixteen charter members. Nine years later Sokol *Blesk* sponsored the first gymnastics meet in Baltimore, but the unit did not own a gymnasium, and lacked qualified instructors. Finally, in 1902, they built their own facility in the heart of the city's "little Bohemia," a hub of Czech activity for forty-eight years. The building had a gymnasium, restaurant, meeting rooms, and a custodian's living quarters. The growth in membership encouraged the formation of a Dramatic Club, and other activities, including talks by noted dignitaries. A new gymnasium was built in 1954, and in 1962 the name of the unit was changed to Sokol Baltimore. Another unit in existence since 1890, *Baltimorská Jednotá Sokolic,* merged with Sokol Baltimore in 1971. After selling the property in 1998, Sokol Baltimore's gymnastic classes were held in St. Patrick Hall, until 2011, when an earthquake damaged the facility. Two years later the unit purchased a building, and within a year, following renovations, the facility was reopened, and activities resumed. Sokol Baltimore is proud that Czechoslovak President Masaryk visited Baltimore in 1918 and was made an honorary member of their Sokol. The unit continues providing gymnastic and fitness programs for youths and adults.

Sokol Tyrš, Cedar Rapids, Iowa. In 1873, a group of twenty-nine men formed *Jednota Tyrš* (Unit Tyrš) as a branch of the Czech Reading Society, an organization founded five years earlier. Sokol *Tyrš* was the second Sokol, after St. Louis, west of the Mississippi. By the time the unit was established, the city already had a significant Czech population. The gymnasts utilized the Reading Society's hall for their training. A second club, Cedar Rapids Sokol, was organized three years later, but merged with Sokol *Tyrš* in 1888. The unit then became Sokol *Tyrš* Cedar Rapids. A house,

purchased in 1892, was converted into a gymnasium, and a women's group was founded that same year. This wooden building was utilized from 1896 until a relatively spacious hall was built in 1901. However, the building was acquired in 1907 by a railroad, because train tracks were being expanded. The unit responded with a fund drive that enabled the construction of a new building in 1909. That building served the Sokols until the flood of 2008. Cedar Rapids Sokol's building, although damaged, endured the flood of 2008, but was sold. That building, which served Sokol for ninety-nine years, was placed on the National Register of Historic Places in 2013. A new training center houses the gymnastic classes that continue to be scheduled.

During the early decades of the 20th century, the Sokol Cedar Rapids gymnasts earned many honors in national competitions, e.g., American Athletic Association, as well as in the 1907 Slet in Prague. A highlight of the unit's gymnastic program was the success of Rudolf Novak, a veteran of World War I, who was selected for the 1924 US Olympic Gymnastics team (see Chapter 5).

Sokol Detroit. This unit was founded in 1875 in response to a notice in the local newspaper calling for a meeting to discuss the formation of a Sokol gymnastic club. Twelve enthusiastic immigrants at that meeting founded Gymnastic Unit Sokol Detroit, and three years later a hall was erected on Detroit's East Side, a section of Detroit that included a sizable Czech community. In 1881, the unit merged with a Czech fraternal organization, Budivoj, and Sokol Detroit then became Sokol Budivoj. Subsequently, some of its members decided to form a new Sokol unit on the West side where many lived, hence Sokol Podlipny was organized in 1889. The unit was named after a Jan Podlipný (1848–1914) a Czech orator, mayor of Prague, and the first president of ČOS (Czech Organization Sokol). A third gymnastics association, Sokol Palacky, which honored the name of Jan Palacký, the Czech historian, was established in 1909 and was part of the District Fuegner-Tyrš, whereas the other units belonged to the larger National Unity Sokol. These units grew and developed strong gymnastics programs. The Podlipny unit outgrew its original home and built the Czech National Hall, which became the main Czech cultural and gymnastics center in Detroit. The

*Slovanská Lípa Hall, Chicago (circa 1871), the home of the
first Sokol in Chicago (Gymnastic Unit Sokol of Chicago) established in 1866.*

Sokol New York (circa 1896)

Podlipny and Palacky units merged in 1916, and then in 1917, Budivoj joined with the two merged units to establish Sokol Detroit, a move that unified the many talents of each of the clubs. In 1934, Sokol Detroit bought land on Sandy Bottom Lake near South Lyon, Michigan, and utilized it for summer camping. As members moved to the suburbs in the late 1950s the Sokol Hall in Detroit's East Side was sold, and a new Sokol Cultural Center was opened in Dearborn Heights in 1967.

East Coast Sokols

Following the establishment of Sokol New York and Svornost in 1867, and Blesk in Baltimore in 1872, Long Island, New York, became the home of Sokol Fuegner in 1876. By 1914, there were three units in Long Island (Fuegner, Bohemia, and East Islip), and units in Philadelphia, Little Ferry, New Jersey, Westfield, Massachusetts, and Newark. Thus, by that year, East Coast had ten Sokol units that were members of the National Union Sokol.

Sokol Little Ferry, New Jersey

In 1896, a group of young immigrants from Bohemia organized a Sokol unit in that city, located just west of New York City. They soon erected a hall and began offering gymnastic classes, which attracted many young people, since it was the first public hall in the city, and because it accepted all nationalities. Some older members organized a "fife and drum corps," which became known throughout the US during the first two decades of the 20th century. Moreover, the unit featured plays (in English and Czech), and organized a choir and orchestra. A women's division of Sokol Little Ferry was created in 1909 and was very active in teaching gymnastics, fund raising, and support of the Czech Free School of Little Ferry. Although a fire destroyed the hall in 1911, a new hall was built a year later and served as a community center, which included the participation of older men in senior exercise classes. Sokol Little Ferry maintained gymnastics classes for all age groups until the last decade. One of its members is a major contributor to the sport of rhythmic gymnastics, as a competitor, organizer, and judge. She is a USA Gymnastics Hall of Fame inductee (see Chapter 5).

Chicago: Hub of Sokol Activity

Greater Chicago has consistently had very large and active units. In 1914, only Sokol New York had more members than the Pilsen and Chicago clubs. By 1933, Sokols Slávský, Chicago, and Havlíček-Tyrš each had more than 500 members, a year when Sokol New York continued to have the largest membership. By that year, membership had grown in most of the urban centers, whereas many smaller towns experienced a decline in membership, as evidenced by those in Menominee and Manitowoc, Wisconsin; Pine City Minnesota; Guy, Texas; and Mandan, North Dakota; with each having fewer than thirty members.

Late 19th Century

The influx of Czech settlers into Chicago precipitated a desire to form Sokol units in their immediate neighborhoods, the first of which was *Tělocvičná Jednota Sokol v Chicagu* (Gymnastic Unit Sokol in Chicago) in 1866. This Sokol group led the way in establishing relationships with the German Turnverein, helped establish the Thalia Dramatic club in 1875, and the unit became the "main focus of Czech social and national life in Chicago" (Bubenicek, 2011, 259). In 1872, this first Sokol in Chicago rented space to the newly established Czech-American Sokol, a unit that merged with the Gymnastic Unit Sokol in Chicago, in 1892, and thereby established Sokol Slavonic Linden/Tabor. It was located at 13th Street and Karlov Avenue in the Merigold neighborhood (also called New Tabor). The merger of the two Sokol clubs then utilized a spacious national building, with a gymnasium, school classroom, ballroom, and stage. Sokol *Čechie,* established in 1877, was located at Halsted and Western Avenue. In 1888, two new Sokol units were founded: Sokol Prague, in the "Praha" neighborhood at 12th Street and Canal, and Sokol Fuegner in Town of Lake, a large region, spanning west from State Street to Harlem, and south from 39th Street to 87th Street. The Praha neighborhood was destroyed by the Great Chicago fire of 1871, and many of its residents then settled in the Pilsen (Plzen) district. By 1893, there were eleven Sokol units in Chicago (Bubenicek, 2011, 392–410).

Sokol Tabor Hall in Chicago's Merigold neighborhood (circa 1892).

Czech-American Sokol Hall, Milwaukee (completed in 1895)

Sokol Pilsen (Plzeňský)

Pilsen Brewery was in the region of the city near Blue Island and 18th Street, a region which became known as the Pilsen district. In 1879, a group of twenty-one men met in Capauch's Tavern and organized a Sokol unit that was named after the neighborhood where it was established. Josef Čermák, served as gymnastics instructor in the new Sokol Pilsen, and was followed by Anton Haller in 1901, a propagator of the Tyrš system and a founder of Sokol units in Bavaria (Bubenicek, 2011, 427–8). Haller established a gymnastics school at Sokol Pilsen, which became a model for other units, and he is also credited with spearheading the development of Pilsen Sokol Camp in New Buffalo Michigan. Sokol Pilsen members helped establish Sokol Town of Lake in 1892. Sokol Pilsen was not only consistent in producing quality gymnasts, but also developed a library and a dramatic group, and helped build Thalia Hall, a center for the arts and entertainment, which is now a National Historic Landmark. Pilsen Sokol founded the first Czech School in Chicago in 1882. In 1895, a three-story high Pilsen Sokol Hall with an indoor swimming pool was built. The membership continued to grow, and at the onset of World War I only Sokol New York had more members than Sokols Pilsen and Chicago. The legendary Jarka Jelinek, a key leader in developing gymnasts and Sokol leaders, was a member of Sokol Pilsen. In 1940, the unit's debts were enough to warrant foreclosure, but an aggressive fund-raising effort erased the debt. However, in 1944 the majestic Sokol Pilsen building was sold to the Polish Falcons.

Sokol Chicago

Two units, Sokols California and Fuegner joined forces in 1892, a move that resulted in the formation of Sokol Chicago, which initially held classes and meetings in a temporary location. Sokol Chicago was instrumental in organizing a Czech school in their neighborhood in 1896. It soon became evident that a building was necessary to provide for the growing gymnastic unit. Consequently, a lot at 2335 Kedzie Avenue, in Czech California, at the western edge of the Pilsen area, was purchased, and in 1899 a building was erected, and an addition completed in 1912. The unit grew, organized a theatrical group and band, and became the center of Czech gymnastic, social, and cultural activities. During the second decade of the early 1900s, Sokol Klatovsky gymnasts trained in Ladmir Hall at 19th and Leavitt Streets, in the Czech California neighborhood, and then merged with Sokol Chicago. In 1923, a summer camp was purchased in St. Charles, Illinois. Sokol Chicago served as a model for other units, because of their outstanding gymnastics program, quality gymnasts at all levels, and large membership. They provided members to every Slet team that competed in Prague, their high division team was unbeaten during a forty-five-year period, and four of their gymnasts became national Sokol champions, and one was a NCAA gymnastic champion and Olympian. They also were known for their volleyball and basketball teams. Because so many of their members had relocated to the suburbs, Sokol Chicago merged with Havlíček-Tyrš and West Suburban in 1993 to form Chicagoland Sokol.

Sokol Tabor

Many mergers of Sokol units, during the last three decades of the 19th century, led to the formation of Sokol Tabor. It was in 1892, as noted earlier, that Sokol Gymnastic Union Sokol in Chicago and Czech-American Sokol merged to form Sokol Slavic Linden in the Merigold neighborhood, which was also known as "New Tabor." Two years earlier a new unit to be called "Tabor" was proposed and established, but its hall, the scene of much gymnastic activity, was destroyed by fire in 1892. Subsequently, the unit was reestablished, and in 1894 a women's auxiliary was formed. In 1914, Tabor merged with Slavic Linden and became "Sokol Tabor-Slovanska Lipa." A year later another fire destroyed the largest portion of their building. Then in 1921, Sokol Slavoj merged with Sokol Tabor-Slavic Linden. However, as more members were moving to Chicago's western suburbs, Sokol Tabor was joined by Sokol Oak Park in 1926 and moved to Berwyn, where Sokol Tabor has continued to be one of the most active and successful Sokols. Their junior and senior women have won numerous gymnastics awards, including National Sokol Championships. Their member, Mildred Prchel, was inducted in the USA Gymnastics Hall of Fame (See Chapter 5).

Sokol Slávský

In February 1890, two Sokol units, Fuegner (most their members were liberal) and Linha (majority of their members were Catholic), decided to put their differences aside and joined together in the Fuegner Hall, where they declared that they were united as Sokol Slávský. The new unit grew quickly; gymnastics programs were developed, and a library was established in 1894. In 1923, Sokol Jonas, named after the Bohemian-American statesman and editor of the *Slave* newspaper in Racine, Wisconsin, merged with Slávský. Karel Jonas Dramatic Association of Cicero, a highly acclaimed theatrical group at the end of World War I, was named after the Bohemian-American statesman and editor of the *Slave* newspaper in Racine, Wisconsin. With the increase in membership, the need for a more spacious building became evident. A successful fund drive led to the construction, in 1925, of a beautiful, spacious building on the corner of Cermak and Lombard Avenue in Cicero, at the cost of one million dollars. The building included a large hall, ballroom, theater, large gymnasium, an Olympic-size swimming pool, and rental space. The new building became the pride of the Czech community. However, financial problems, caused by the Great Depression, forced Sokol Slávský to sell their building. Fortunately, it was purchased by the Czechoslovak Society of America, and Sokol was able to continue using the facility. After celebrating Slávský's 90th anniversary in 1980, the building was sold and Sokol gymnastic classes were held in the deactivated Piper School in Berwyn for eight years, and then beginning in 1989, in a church gymnasium. Finally, in 1995, Sokols Slávský and Berwyn merged. Members of Sokol Slávský were very active in a vigorous gymnastics program and in other sports. The unit was highly visible, provided leadership, and consistently contributed to the administrations of the Central District and the American Sokol Organization.

Sokol Havlíček-Tyrš

In 1903, Sokol Tyrš was founded in Chicago's Czech California neighborhood, and gymnastic classes were initiated in a hall owned by a Sokol member. A year later Sokol Havlíček was established and a site was purchased on 28th and Trumbull Ave, and then, in 1907, a lot was purchased on Lawndale Avenue at 26th Street. However, the two new units enjoyed a short independent tenure, because they agreed to merge, and Sokol Havlíček-Tyrš came into existence in 1911. The unit opened a new building that same year on the Lawndale property. The gymnasium was the largest of all the Sokols at the time. An influx of many Czech immigrants into the neighborhood resulted in a steadily increasing membership. Moreover, Sokol Havlíček-Tyrš gained more members when Sokol Vysehrad merged with it in 1914, and again when Sokol Komensky joined in 1921. Havlíček-Tyrš thrived for many years and was characterized by an active gymnastic program. Moreover, their hall was a center for neighborhood activities, which included plays and various festivals. For thirty years the unit owned Camp Lidice in Crystal Lake, about fifty miles northwest of Chicago, but the camp was sold in 1970 due to a decline in usage. Then in 1974, the Sokol Havlíček-Tyrš building was severely damaged by an electrical storm and sold, which required the unit to hold meetings at Sokol Berwyn. The unit merged with Sokols West Suburban and Chicago to form Sokol Chicagoland in 1993. Many Sokols who joined units in Chicago's suburbs were trained at Havlíček-Tyrš.

Sokol Town of Lake

Two Sokol units formed in the late 19th century, Prague in 1888 and Pokrok, (meaning progress) in 1893, merged in 1916 and became Sokol Town of Lake, taking the name of their community. Prior to the merger, the Prague and Pokrok Sokols utilized various halls for their activities. *Česko-Národní* (Czech-National) Sokol had joined Sokol Pokrok earlier, and both units had strong gymnastic programs. By naming the new unit "Sokol Town of Lake" the largely Czech community, which valued and supported Sokol training, was honored. *Šibřinky,* an annual costume ball, was not only a popular social event, but served as a source of funding, and is credited with helping establish a summer camp at Willow Springs, Illinois. The unit grew, and after World War I, Sokol Town of Lake had several outstanding instructors. Moreover, the unit was very active in dramatics, summer camping, and social functions. During the 1920s, membership reached 500, and every branch of Sokol, e.g., gymnastics, dramatics, and camping, had qualified leaders. Gymnastic activity continued, uninterrupted, for many decades. Many talented gymnasts and instructors were developed, and included many women, who had their own organization since 1891. The sale of the School Hall, utilized by the Sokol, and the move to the suburbs of many of the unit's members resulted in a sharp decline in the unit's activities.

Suburban Chicago Units

With the migration of Czechs to Chicago's suburbs, not surprisingly, new Sokol units were established in these settlements. As previously noted, Slávský and Tabor Sokols moved from Chicago to Cicero and Berwyn, respectively. These communities were becoming major Czech settlements. Other suburban units were established, joined American Sokol Organization, and subsequently many found mergers to be beneficial, especially during the late 20th century.

Sokol Berwyn. Organized in 1911, this unit was able to erect a building a year later. By 1913, a dramatic society and a choral group were in place, and later a Czech school was established. A new gymnasium was added to the building in 1924. A women's unit was established in 1925, but, merged with the men's unit in 1944. Stanley Matoska, a member of the Czech gymnastic team, settled in the US and taught gymnastics at Sokol Berwyn for many years. Later, Stanley Barcal, a champion gymnast from Sokol Chicago, taught at the unit for thirty years. Ellen Schnabl established one of the first Sokol pre-school (tots) gym classes. In order to increase its activity the unit merged in 1995 with Sokol Slávský, and took the name "Berwyn-Slávský."

Sokol Stickney. Organized in 1928, this unit utilized a neighborhood facility until 1936, when a building was constructed. Lacking adequate funds during this Great Depression period, the Sokol members used bricks from demolished structures in Chicago, and transported them to Stickney. Labor for construction was provided, mainly, by the unit's members. The building was remodeled in 1970 and new equipment was purchased. Sokol Stickney is especially proud of its role in combating juvenile delinquency by their gymnastics program, and the leadership of their well-trained instructors. In 2018, Sokol Stickney was renamed "United."

Sokol Brookfield. Another unit that overcame the obstacles of the Great Depression was Sokol Brookfield.

Because of the dedication of the Czech Club of Brookfield members, who envisioned a center for Czech culture and activities, a cornerstone was laid for the *Národní Síň* (National Hall) in 1929, and two years later, the Sokol Brookfield Gymnastics Organization was founded. Gymnastics classes began immediately, and membership increased. After years of limited activity in the 1930s, the unit became stronger and joined the American Sokol Organization (ASO) in 1940. In 1946, its name was changed to Sokol Brookfield Educational Institute. In 2005, Sokol Brookfield merged with Sokol Berwyn-Slávský.

Sokol West Suburban. This unit in Downers Grove was established in 1960 to accommodate a community that had developed over the last decade. However, they joined Havlíček-Tyrš and Chicago in a merger to create Sokol Chicagoland in 1993.

Sokol Spirit. This very active unit in Brookfield, Illinois, was formed in 2005, when Sokols Berwyn-Slávský and Brookfield merged. Berwyn-Slávský was established in 1995 when Sokol Slávský (founded in 1890) merged with Sokol Berwyn, a unit that was established in 1911. Sokol Spirit continued the tradition of a strong exercise program developed in Sokol Slávský by Ann Halik. This program draws fitness-minded seniors from many Sokol units in Greater Chicago.

Sokol Naperville Tyrš (Illinois). Linda Filipello and her family founded a new Sokol unit in Naperville in 1983, because many families were interested in a Sokol gym closer to their homes. Although the new unit was chartered in 1984, funds for a building were not available, thus Filipello contacted schools in the district. During the first year, classes were held in an elementary school, and subsequently at Naperville North High School and Naperville Central High School, because these schools had dedicated gymnastics facilities. The first-year classes included twenty-five students and two instructors, and the use of very little equipment. The second-year classes at North High School had an enrollment of 144 students and six instructors, which included a former Turnverein coach. Funds for equipment are currently donated to the high school by Sokol Naperville. By offering gymnastics classes in this large Chicago suburb, the sport of gymnastics has survived in the district's high schools,

Above: *Sokol Pilsen, Chicago (circa 1895–1900)*

Following Page: *Sokol Chicago: original building, circa 1899 (top) and after addition, circa 1912 (bottom)*

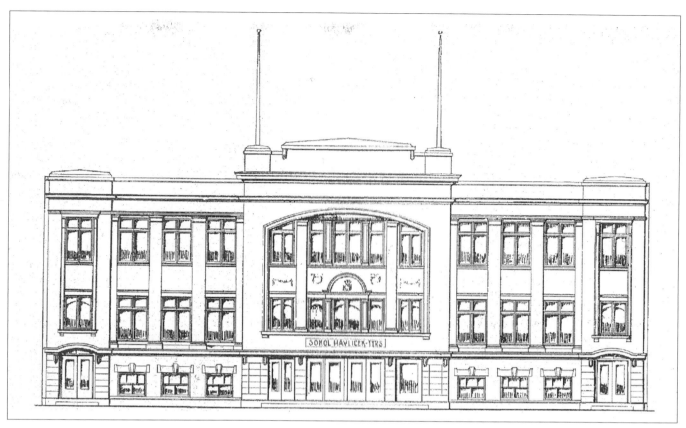

Sokol Havlíček-Tyrš, Chicago. This sketch illustrates their building erected in 1911.

while it has disappeared from most of the other high schools in Chicagoland. Currently, classes are scheduled three times per week, and the instructors are former gymnasts. Sokol Naperville sponsors gymnastics competitions for private clubs, which helps the unit's costs of operation.

Sokol Chicagoland, Downers Grove, Illinois. This unit was founded in 1993 when Sokols Havlíček-Tyrš, Chicago and West Suburban merged their memberships. Gymnastic instruction is provided one evening per week. Sokol Chicagoland along with the Central District of ASO sponsors gymnasts at the Elite Sports Complex.

Czech Cleveland

Cleveland has a rich Czech history, with immigrant settlements dating back to the mid-nineteenth century. Czech culture was established in neighborhoods given Czech names, such as *Zizkov* (a district of Prague), *Praha,* and *na Vršku* (on the hill). These neighborhoods were rich in Czech culture and were aided by the many benevolent and fraternal societies. Ledbetter (1919) wrote about the Czechs in Cleveland

and noted the formation of Sokol Units, and the building of halls that served as gymnasiums and cultural-social centers. The first Sokol group in Cleveland began as an affiliation of the Perun club, which was the dramatic wing of *Slovanská Lípa (Pamatník Sokola Pražského,* 1883, 293–4). In 1870, *Perun* built an all-purpose hall that served as a school, theater and gymnasium.

Sokol Perun/Cleveland. Thus, the first Cleveland Sokol was established by *Perun* in 1870, and for the first year Sokol utilized the *Perun* Hall for training before they moved to the new National Hall provided by *Slovanská Lípa.* Later, the Sokols returned to *Perun* Hall, and in 1880 they officially became Sokol Unit Cleveland. However, the unit was dissolved in 1888, when the *Perun* club folded. As noted below, Sokol Cleveland was re-established in 1895.

Cleveland's five original Sokol units. In 1879, Sokol *Čech* (Czech), later known as Czech Sokol, was established, and was followed by the birth of *Nová Vlast* (New Homeland) in 1893 and then the rebirth of Sokol Cleveland in 1895. Cleveland's fourth unit, Havlíček began in 1907 and its fifth unit, Tyrš, opened its doors in 1919. Czech and Havlíček joined to become Čech-Havlíček in 1921. Sokol Cleveland bought their original hall in 1910 in the eastern section of the city, and a new hall in 1946. However, fourteen years later the unit merged with Czech-Havlíček, and became Sokol Cleveland Čech-Havlíček, a merger that lasted until 1985, the year the unit was disbanded. Many of its members then joined Sokol Greater Cleveland. When Sokol Tyrš originated it took the name "Jan Ámos Komenský," in honor of the famous Czech educator, but in 1926 the name was changed to Sokol Tyrš. That year the unit organized a drama group, sewing circle, and concert band. In 1923, Cleveland Sokols purchased a camp in Twinsburg Ohio, which they named Sokol Fresh Air Camp. The site was not only for camping, but also hosted Sokol schools, district exhibitions, and cabins for Sokol members.

Sokol Čech-Havlíček. The merger of the two units in 1921 (Čech and Havlíček) led to further success in gymnastics. Frank Prihoda, an accomplished gymnast from Czechoslovakia, joined the unit in 1925 and taught all classes for one year. He then left to become the instructor of Sokol St. Louis. Subsequently, the technical board provided the gymnastics instruction and held classes from 6:30–10:30 pm Monday—Friday and on Sunday mornings. In 1926, a "Junior's Club" was launched.

Sokol Tyrš. Founded in 1919 as Sokol Jan Komensky, this unit changed its name to Sokol Tyrš in 1926, and a new hall was opened in 1927. This Sokol had a very active gymnastics program, and their members won numerous prizes in both Sokol and non-Sokol competitions. In 1969, they had 331 adult members and 191 gymnasts. Many of their members completed instructor's courses and taught the unit's classes. Sokol Tyrš hosted many groups, e.g., a concert band, sewing club and theater group. In 1976, Sokol Tyrš incorporated *Nová Vlast,* a merger that became Sokol Greater Cleveland.

Nová Vlast (New Country) and Česka Sin (hall). The hall, a Sokol historic landmark, accommodated West Side Sokols. Built in 1890, it was purchased in 1907 by a group of Czech lodges, including Sokol *Nová Vlast,* which equipped the hall for gymnastics and held classes there. *Nová Vlast* established a

gymnastics club in 1892 with thirty-eight young members, a slate of officers, and a gymnastics instructor. The unit built their first hall in 1893, which they utilized until their move to *Česka Sin.* Bohemian National Hall on Cleveland's East Side was built in 1896 and is now on the National Register of Historic Places. When *Nová Vlast* and Tyrš Sokols merged they formed American Sokol Inc., and they deeded the hall to the new organization: Sokol Greater Cleveland Gymnastics and Educational Organization. By 1985, 250 children attended gymnastic classes at Sokol Greater Cleveland. The success and growth of this organization led to expansion of the National Hall, in 2000, that provided a separate athletic facility and the addition of a museum. Cleveland's Czech history supports the conclusion that the Sokols played a central role in the city's ethnic culture by maintaining quality gymnastic programs, as well as theater, and a multitude of social and cultural activities.

Sokol Greater Cleveland. The mergers that gave birth to this large and active unit, in 1976, brought together a talented board of instructors, and provided a better financial base and overall better efficiency of operation. Sokol Greater Cleveland represents a good model for Sokol units, where mergers, if practical, represent the best chance for viability of Sokol programs. Sokol Greater Cleveland currently has 402 members, and 210 individuals, aged 3–85 years, participate in their gymnastics programs. Their classes include tots, boys and girls, junior boys and girls, men, women, as well as fitness activities for seniors. There are about eight students each month that participate in an aerial circus arts program. The unit also hosts a Czech and Sokol Museum and a library. Cultural activities include dances, concerts, a Czech Holiday Fair, and dinners.

Westward Migration and Further Midwestern Development

As noted in Chapter 3, Czech immigrants began settling in the Midwest during the late 19th century. They came because of the job opportunities in the cities, and, most often, because of the available farmland. Figure 3, based on the 1900 US Census, indicates that 25% of Czech immigrants lived in

Cleveland's Bohemian National Hall, built in 1896, is on the National Register of Historic Places. It was expanded in 2000 and is the home of Sokol Greater Cleveland.

Sokol Cleveland: men gymnasts (circa 1900)

Illinois, most of whom settled in Chicago. The other midwestern states with the greatest percentage of Czechs were Nebraska, Ohio, Wisconsin, Minnesota, and Iowa. Not surprisingly, many Sokol units were established in these states. Midwestern cities with large Czech communities, e.g., Cleveland, Chicago, Detroit, Omaha, and St. Paul all formed Sokol units. However, the vast number of small towns that followed suit provides the best evidence of the strong desire of these Czech immigrants to form Sokol units for the purpose of fitness, and as cultural centers for their families.

Wisconsin

Kewaunee. A group of young Czech immigrants organized a Sokol unit in 1878 and then bought the Kewaunee *Slovanská Lípa* Hall, where gymnastics, theater, and other cultural events were held. In 1914, the unit erected a brick building, but did not have the funds to support the costs of the new facility. Thus, the building was sold, and the unit was dissolved.

Racine. Not surprisingly, Racine, a Wisconsin town with a high percentage of Czechs, developed a Sokol unit when seventeen young men began practicing gymnastics in a barn in 1889. Thus, Sokol *Mladočech* (young Czech) was established two years later, with the purchase of a building that they named "Bohemian Turner Hall," consistent with the idea that "turning" describes gymnastics routines, rather than to imply that it was a German club. Racine Sokols sponsored the formation of a new Sokol unit in the small farming town of Caledonia in 1894, which took the name of "Sokol Tabor." However, the unit was active for only twenty-six years. Sokol *Mladočech* affiliated with the *Fügner-Tyrš* District, a rival organization of the National Union of Sokols. *Fügner-Tyrš* District units were called "red" Sokols, because they utilized Czech language for gymnastics instruction and distinguished themselves as true Czech Sokols by their red colored uniforms. The unit remained active after the *Fügner-Tyrš* District united with ASO, but disbanded by 2000.

Manitowoc. This town was home to the *Slovanská Lípa* Opera House, an expensive three-story building opened in 1886; a year later Manitowoc Sokol acquired joint-ownership and equipped a gymnasium in the building, which also featured a library, kitchen, and dining room. It was the center of Czech culture and hosted balls, dances, a music club, and high school graduations (Laska, 1978, 98–100). The men's gymnastics team from Manitowoc won a championship at the 1904 National Slet. The building, like that of many Sokols, was a cultural center and the site of balls, concerts, and plays. In addition to the gymnasium, the hall had an auditorium, which hosted a drama club, and various social events.

Other Wisconsin towns. Melnik Sokol was organized at the end of World War I and held training sessions in a small hall attached to a grocery store and tavern. Rosecrans Sokols trained in another hall, and merged with Sokol Melnik in the 1930s. New units were formed in the 1930s in Cadott, Haugen, Phillips, and Polivka Corners. In order to accommodate the performance of giant swings on the horizontal bar, in the Polivka Corners Sokol, a trap door was installed in the low ceiling and opened during gymnastic practices. Thus, the legs of a gymnast's body were in the attic during a giant swing (see Figure 4). Sokol Haugen was established by a ZCBJ Lodge (Western Fraternal Bohemian Association) in that town, but was active for only eighteen years. The unit was recognized for its numerous Czech language dramas.

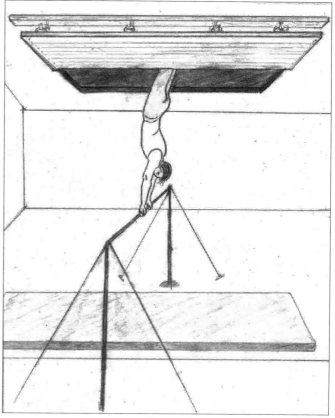

Figure 4

Above: *Sokol Slavic Linden Manitowoc (circa 1886)*

Opposite Page: *Figure 4. Polivka Corners, Wisconsin had a Sokol gymnasium with a relatively low ceiling. To accommodate the performance of giant swings on the horizontal bar, the ceiling was opened, and a trap door installed.*

Minnesota

Sokol Minnesota. A Sokol unit was established in St. Paul in 1882, through the efforts of ten visionary men. The first few years of the unit were difficult because of a lack of equipment and instructors. The classes were small, but the Sokols formed a close association with the German Turners, which helped the unit in its development. The new Sokol in St. Paul adopted the name "Sokol Zizka" in 1885 in honor of Jan Zizka (1374–1424), a national Bohemian military commander who defeated the invading German knights. Unfortunately, their original wooden building was destroyed by fire in 1886. Then four years later Sokol St. Paul disbanded. However, with the arrival of more Czech immigrants, a new St. Paul Sokol unit was formed in 1900, and within six years a women's auxiliary was in place. The CSPS (Czech Slovak Protective Society) Hall, built in 1887, served as a gymnasium, and since 1977 has been on the list of National Register of Historical Places. With the formation of Sokol units in other Minnesota towns and cities, a District of Minnesota Sokols was created in 1915. Then these units formed the Northern District of the National Union Sokol. A Sokol camp was developed in Pine City in 1926. However, most of the units became inactive so that in 1971, Sokol St. Paul was the lone active Sokol in the Northern District, and for that reason joined the Western District. Sokol St. Paul became Sokol Minnesota in 1978, and obtained sole ownership of the CSPS Hall. The unit remains active and hosts gymnastics classes and competitions, classes in Czech language and culture, and many social celebrations. A nursery gymnastics class for tots, aged 2–5 years and a co-ed adult gymnastics class were innovations many decades ago.

Other Minnesota towns. Sokols were founded in Hopkins, New Prague, Pine City, Owatonna, and Meadowlands. These new units were established with the help of Sokol St. Paul.

Michigan, Ohio, and Western Pennsylvania

In addition to Detroit, Sokol units were also established in Saginaw, Owosso, Azalia, and Banister, Michigan. In Ohio, outside Cleveland's Czech neighborhoods, there were Sokol units in Toledo, Twinsburg, and Lorain.

Sokol Moravan, Toledo. A group of young immigrants, from a southern region of Moravia, organized this unit in 1909. From its birth, Sokol Moravan prided itself in its enthusiasm for gymnastics, a life of fellowship, and its financial support for the club. A gymnasium was erected in 1931, and survived despite the financial difficulties of the decade.

Sokol Rip (Pittsburg), and Sokol Irwin. These two units, like Sokol Moravan, were members of the Northeastern District. Rip was established in 1881 as an affiliate of Club Slovoj. For many years Rip's gymnasts trained in the German Turner Hall, but in 1888 the Sokol unit helped build the Czech National Hall in Pittsburg. Sokol Irwin, established in 1915, was located about twenty-seven miles southeast of Pittsburg.

Omaha and Small towns in Nebraska and Iowa

As railroads expanded westward, Omaha became a "springboard" to smaller Czech centers in Nebraska, which were founded in the late 19th century (Laska 1978, 24). These immigrant settlements continued their Czech culture by establishing fraternal organizations, one of which was Sokol. These organizations co-operated in their efforts in developing and maintaining the Czech culture. Characteristic of Czech-American public halls, those built in Nebraska after 1900 included a bona fide stage for dramatic performance; ZCBJ and Sokol organizations built most of the stages, and their architectural designs symbolized the Czech identity.

Sokol Omaha. Frank Jelen, a Czech immigrant, was one of the founders of Sokol Svornost (1867) in Morrisania New York; he then moved to Omaha's "Little Bohemia" in 1876. Sokol was evidently his priority, because a year after he moved to Omaha, he invited twenty young men, including his son, to his home where they discussed the need for a Sokol unit in their Czech neighborhood. The next day, (September 3, 1877) they formed a Sokol unit, and identified officers and a gymnastic instructor. Initially, gymnastic classes were held in the Metz Brewery Hall, but in 1892 a fund drive began and raised enough money to build a Sokol Hall in 1899. Sokol Omaha Women's Unit was formed in that year, a Czech School in 1895, and the Sokol Tyrš Dramatic Society in 1914. Demands for a larger building led to a fund drive and the construction of Sokol Auditorium in 1926. A key factor in the fund drive was that each member contributed. The facility included a gymnasium, hall for theater and dances, and meeting rooms; the six-lane bowling alley, and regular public dances helped support the unit financially. Moreover, a 1923 bazaar contributed $13,000, and another $30,000 was raised subsequently; the mortgage was fully paid, twenty years after the building's construction. A second women's group (Unit Sokol Tyrš) was organized in 1899. Their group trained together with Sokol Omaha Women's Unit, in the same facility, thus in 1948 they finally merged.

Sokol Omaha Auditorium was a cultural center for Czech-Americans. Czech plays and school promoted the native language, and twenty-five fraternal lodges met there regularly. The Sokol Dramatic Society was active for about ninety years and featured dramas, comedies, and musicals including operettas. Many cultural groups met there regularly, e.g., mother's club, sewing circle, and book club. The latter was held in the well-stocked Serpan Library, which also served as a meeting room. Adjacent to the bowling alley was a bar and card rooms that were gathering places for many in the Czech community. Sokol Camp was established in 1936 and provided summer camping for youth and lots for members enabling them to build cottages. This is one example of how a Sokol Unit was a hub in a community, and promoted and facilitated both culture and gymnastics. Another asset was that during much of Sokol Omaha's existence, a full-time gymnastics instructor was available. Two Sokol Omaha trained gymnasts were members of US Olympic teams in the 1980s, and are inductees of the US Hall of Fame (see Chapter 5).

Sokol South Omaha. A second Czech community in Omaha developed in South Omaha (now a part of the City of Omaha) in the Brown Park region. In 1888, the Gymnastic Sokol Society *Fügner-Tyrš* was established, and was followed by the formation of a women's unit, *Sbor Sokolek Libuše,* South Omaha in 1902. *Libuše* was a Czech queen who prophesized Prague as a great city, and helped found the city. The two units initially utilized Beseda Hall for training, but then in 1909 they became co-owners of the Bohemian National Hall, where their gymnastic classes were held. Already in 1890, the unit's gymnasts were participating in gymnastic competitions. A second, short lived, gymnastic unit (Tyrš) was formed, but merged with Sokol South Omaha in 1909. The wood structure, which also served as a gathering place for cultural activities, was destroyed by fire in 1975, but gymnastic activity con-tinued by utilizing a junior high school, as well as Sokol Omaha. Within two years the destroyed hall was replaced by a new building in the same location. Sokol Park was developed along the Platte River after Sokol purchased land in 1936, and has been utilized for camping, dances, picnics, and other recreational activities. During the last few decades of the 20th century, Sokol South Omaha was one of the dominating Sokol units in competitive gymnastics, and the home of many American Sokol Organization Instructor's Schools. The unit developed a Sokol Museum that exhibited thousands of items. However, in 2014 the building was sold, and gymnastics classes are being held at Sokol Omaha.

Many Sokols in small Nebraska towns. The first National Unity units, in 1894, were organized in four districts (Appendix A). The Western District consisted of eleven units, of which eight were in Nebraska, two in Iowa, and one in Missouri (St. Louis). Sokols were found in the small towns of Bruno, Crete, Wilber, Linwood, Plattsmouth, and Schuyler in Nebraska, and Oxford Junction in Iowa. By 1907, the Western District consisted of seventeen Sokol units, of which eleven were in small eastern Nebraska towns. However, ten years later, Bruno, Linwood, and Oxford Junction were no longer active, but six new units were established in Nebraska: Abie, Dodge, Clarkson, Howells, Ord, and Ravenna (Appendix B). The success in establishing Sokol units in small towns demonstrates the creativeness of Czech settlers and their desire for community centers that featured gymnastics, Czech culture, and socialization. Small towns in other states also accepted the challenge to establish Sokol units, for example Lucas, Wilson, Timken, Vysehrad, and Black Wolf, Kansas. The long-lasting droughts and Great Depression of the 1930s caused many units to close due to the consequential financial difficulties.

Sokol Wilber. A large contingent of Czech immigrants settled in Wilber, a small farming town in southeast Nebraska, where in 1880 they organized a Sokol unit. Their meetings and gymnastics training were held in the Wilber Opera house until 1891 when they built their own hall. After a period of inactivity, the unit reorganized in 1901. Subsequently, they sold their building in order to support the World War I effort. Their attempts to reorganize were initially unsuccessful. However, in 1925 a few inspired members led a reorganization effort that resulted in a

Sokol Omaha Auditorium dedicated in 1926 (circa 1936)

functional unit and new leadership. A new hall was built in 1930, and an addition was completed in 1947, which included a bar and kitchen. The unit was active in gymnastics, Czech School, operettas, and dances. Their Sokol Dramatic Club was organized in 1930, and played a key role in the cultural identity of the city of Wilber. Sokol Wilber maintained its gymnastics programs into the 1980s, and in 1998 their building was placed on the National Registry of Historic places. Wilber is recognized as the "Czech Capital of the US."

Sokol Crete. Another small town Sokol unit that endured the years is Crete, a town just ten miles from Wilber. Gymnastic Unit Sokol Crete was organized in 1884 with eleven founding members, and eight years later Sokol Libuse, a women's gymnastics organization, was established. Czech cultural activities, including meetings of the Bohemian Reading society, were originally conducted in John Svoboda's barn, located midway between Crete and Wilber. Nearby was another building known as Kovarik's hall. It was there that Sokol Crete was organized. The Crete Sokol Hall, a wooden building, built in 1891, was destroyed by fire in 1913, but two years later it was replaced by a new building in the town's center, designed and built by a Moravian and his sons. This building, on the National

Registry of Historic Places since 2003, has been a home for gymnastics, theater, and cultural activities. Sokol Crete was known for theatrical productions, and its stage curtains and scenery flats that were painted by an artist. The building's auditorium and gymnasium were utilized, for several years, by local schools, because they lacked these facilities. Sokol Crete's gymnasts were successful in gymnastics competitions for many years.

Sokol Schuyler (pronounced Sky-ler). Another small Nebraska town that maintained a Sokol unit for a long duration (1891–1977) was Schuyler (correspondence from Joan Sedlacek). The determination and success of the members of this unit is documented by the willingness of young gymnasts to walk thirteen miles (one-way) in order to compete in a gymnastic meet. Moreover, Sokol Schuyler scheduled gymnastics training at 9 p.m. in order to accommodate the working schedules of its members. The unit used the CSPS Hall for classes, and in 1901 merged with a Czech literary and dramatic society.

Sokols in Iowa towns. Cedar Rapids, as noted earlier, was the major Czech Sokol and culture center in Iowa. By 1894, Oxford Junction had established a Sokol, and later units were formed in Iowa City and Marshalltown, but these units were short-lived.

Emergence of Sokol Units in the Southern District

Sokol units in Texas and Oklahoma were first established in the early 20th century, as more immigrants from Bohemia and Moravia settled in the cities and towns, especially in the Dallas/Fort Worth area.

Sokol Karel Havlíček Borovský, Ennis, Texas

While there is some indication of a Sokol unit in Texas (T. J. Sokol Čech-Moravian) as early as 1891, the unit apparently was short-lived. Thus, Havlíček Borovský, Ennis, is recognized as the first Sokol unit in that state. It was organized in 1908 by twenty-two men, and honors the name of a brave journalist and publisher known to be the fearless founder of Czech journalism, and who was esteemed in Bohemia. Originally the gymnastic classes were held in the Slavonic Benevolent Order of the State of Texas National Hall, but a fund drive and donated labor facilitated the construction of a Sokol building that opened in 1913. This first building was destroyed by fire within two years and a second facility experienced the same fate. A third building erected in 1917, served the unit for nineteen years, but was condemned, due to the need of costly repairs. Despite these obstacles the Ennis Sokol survived, and established a library in 1926, and built a fourth gymnasium in 1936, which was utilized for thirty-five years. With a growing number of members, the facility was too small, a concern that precipitated a fund drive and the opening of a new Sokol Gymnastic Center in 1971. Then in 1990 fire struck again, and gym classes were held in rented facilities. Despite the loss of its fifth building, Ennis Sokol hosted the 1990 District Slet, and adopted the slogan: "The spirit remains strong," which so appropriately defined the determination of the Sokol Ennis members. Not surprisingly, a new building, the Sokol Activity Center, was opened in 1991. The unit's history indicates that gymnastics has been its backbone, but that close associations with other Czech organizations, and the inclusion of many cultural events, were also valued. Many fraternal and cultural associations made Sokol Ennis their home, which indicates that it served as a community center. Karel Havlíček Borovsky Sokol was honored in 1989 by the Gymnastics Association of the State of Texas for its "Service to Youth," and for eighty years of continuous gymnastic training. This unit continued growing and remained active in gymnastics and other Sokol activities. By 1979, the Ennis Sokol listed 855 members and 250 attending gymnastics classes. These data attest to the sustainability of this Ennis Sokol, which few Sokols have.

Many Texas Cities and Towns Establish Sokol Units

By 1909, Sokol units had been organized in Shiner, Hallettsville, and Granger. Others followed in Waco, Dallas, Ft. Worth, Penelope, Guy, Seaton, Buckholts, Houston, Crosby, Rowena, Galveston, Corpus Christi, Placedo, Floresville, San Antonio, and East Bernard. These units comprised the Southern District of the ASO. In 1930, fourteen units of the original twenty remained active in Texas. Oklahoma Sokols in Oklahoma City, Yukon, Caldwell, Lucas, and Prague, and Sokol in Wilson, Kansas, were members of the Southwestern District. In 2018, seven units were still active: Ennis, Dallas, Ft. Worth, West, Houston, Corpus Christi in Texas, and Karel Havlíček in Yukon, Oklahoma (Appendix F).

Sokol Zizka, Dallas. Seventeen immigrants met in the home of V. Rezek on January 1, 1912, for the purpose of organizing a Sokol gymnastic unit. Like St. Paul, three decades earlier, the Dallas unit was named after Jan Zižka (1376–1424), a military commander and national Bohemian hero who led the Hussite armies, and defeated the German Knights who had attacked Bohemia. The Sokol organizers elected officers on that day, and initially held gymnastic training in Rezek's backyard. A women's unit *Sokoly Libuse* was established within a year. The members formed an orchestra to raise funds and provided the unit with a library. As a result of the successful fund drive, a hall with a gymnasium, stage, and kitchen was constructed and completed in 1916, and became a center for Czech activities in the city. Although gymnastic activity was a center piece of this unit, as evidenced by the success of their gymnasts, Czech cultural programs and activities were also notable. An orchestra consisting of Sokol members was organized and literary and social activities were frequent. This facility served Sokol Zizka until 1959 when a new building, the Sokol and SPJST (Slavonic Benevolent Order of the State of

Texas) Gymnasium and Recreation Center, was opened. This was the first totally air conditioned Sokol facility in the US. Sokol Zizka Dallas remains active by offering classes in gymnastics, tumbling, karate, and Czech language. It is considered a progressive athletic and educational organization, and is honored to have one of their own earn a spot on the 1980 US Olympic team (see Chapter 5).

Sokol Ft. Worth. This unit is known as "Sokol Center–Fort Worth" a name that fits one of the most active Sokols in the US. Founded in 1912, the unit has been home to many aspiring gymnasts and leaders in the sport in Texas. The programs offered in Sokol Fort Worth are led by certified instructors and are available for all age groups. This unit is a role model for others, as it attests to the value of a good business program, facilities, and staff. Gymnastics classes are offered six days per week, twelve months per year. Training is available for all levels of difficulty, and classes are available for parents and tykes (three years and under), pre-school, boys and girls, juniors, and seniors. Par Khor and tumbling classes are offered, and the unit also sponsors camps for certification of instructors, and eleven to twelve summer swim and gym camps. Sokol Fort Worth employs a full-time General Manager and eleven part-time employees. This progressive Sokol has played a major role in establishing gymnastic programs throughout the state and promoting the sport via the involvement of its members in national and international competitions (see Chapter 5).

Sokol Houston. In 1914, a Sokol group asked a fraternal lodge to use their facilities, and apparently corresponds to the informal formation of Sokol Houston. During World War I activity was suspended until 1919, but it was in 1923 that the organization received the impetus that it needed. John Kasper, a Czech Sokol immigrant, came to Houston and met with some Sokols there. He agreed to help formally establish Sokol Houston, and in 1923 a charter was given to the unit by the American Sokol Organization. Progress in the gym was rapid, as evidenced by Sokol Houston women and men winning first place medals in the Southern District Slet in 1926. During the Great Depression, the gym was not active until 1939. In 1946, Josef Kos, a 1912 Czech Olympian, arrived and became the unit's president. Sokol Houston's first build-ing was erected in 1951, mainly by the members who volunteered their labor. Their second building was completed in 1967.

Sokol West. One of the newest Sokols in the US, West became a reality after a few organization meetings in 1979, and during the next year gymnastic classes were held in what is now St. Mary's gym. In 1989, the construction of Sokol West Gymnasium was completed, however on April 17, 2013 an explosion at a nearby fertilizer company destroyed the Sokol building. This tragedy did not diminish the determination and resilience of the town's Sokol members. What emerged was a well-organized fundraising effort that resulted in the construction of a 12,500 square foot building that opened in 2015. Contributions came not only from all over the US, but also from the Czech government. Petr Gandalovic, the Czech Ambassador, noted that the bond with West Texas and the Czech Republic was strengthened by responding to a tragedy.

Kansas and Oklahoma

Sokol Karel Jonas, Wilson Kansas. Established in 1897, this unit, like several others, was named after Karel Jonas, an early settler in Racine, Wisconsin, who published a newspaper and became a statesman. Sokol members raised funds in order to build a two-story opera house, called Turner Hall, that contained a fully equipped gymnasium. The hall, built of limestone, had incurred a high debt and was in danger of foreclosure. To save the valued hall, CSPS and some other lodges became joint owners. Many gymnasts trained in the hall, especially between 1925 and 1935. However, the gym portion of the opera house was converted into a museum in 1979.

Sokol, Caldwell, Kansas. In 1928, twenty-four charter members founded Sokol Caldwell, and soon the new unit began gymnastics classes in the ZCBJ Hall. After a fire destroyed the building, the unit built a hall of their own, where they held their gymnastic class, and presented both Czech and English plays. Sokol Caldwell, along with three Oklahoma units, and two other Kansas clubs joined the newly formed Southwestern District in 1937.

Sokol Karel Havlíček, Yukon, Oklahoma. An example of cultural preservation can be seen in Yukon Oklahoma, where in 1899 members of this Sokol unit joined with Western Fraternal Life Lodge, Jan Ziska, and erected a community hall which has served as a social center, and lodge meetings, Czech plays, Czech language classes, and dances.

Sokol Reaches the West Coast

In 1904, San Francisco established the first Sokol unit on the West Coast, and five years later Sokol Los Angeles was founded. The Pacific District was formed during the next two decades and included San Francisco, Los Angeles, and Oakland, California, and Scio, Portland, and Malin, Oregon. Finally, in 1940, Fresno, California, became the last unit added to the Pacific District. The units were active in many cultural pursuits, e.g., theater, and social functions. Interest in gymnastics was cultivated in 1914 when ASO instructor Karel Dvorak came to the West Coast and helped spark an increase in membership. Children's summer camps were held in Yosemite and the High Sierras. By 1995, only Los Angeles, San Francisco, and Fresno remained active.

Sokol San Francisco. During the first eight years of the unit's existence, gymnastic classes were held in a Turnverein Hall. However, in 1912, a Sokol Hall was constructed and was utilized until 1968, when a new building was purchased in San Mateo. That building was used by many other Czech and Slovak organizations and served as a center for many Sokol and patriotic activities. Currently, the unit does not have a gymnastics program, but offers senior walks for health combined with socialization.

Sokol Los Angeles. Established in 1909, this West Coast unit first met in a small wood structure, and then in 1928 several Czech and Slovak groups were organized under the umbrella of the "Czechoslovak Patronat." By 1933, construction began on a two-story Czechoslovakian Hall, with a ballroom, dining area, and library, and was utilized by Czech and Slovak groups. The building was located in a developing family housing neighborhood, thus it was sold and a building (Sokol Hall) was purchased by Sokol and *Kroužek Pilná Ruka,* a Czech cultural organization, in 1949, and remodeled in 1955. Sokol hall was a welcoming cultural center for Czech and Slovak immigrants who settled in the Los Angeles area after 1948 and 1968. Support for these recent arrivals was an essential function of Sokol Los Angeles. In 2003, the hall was sold, due to high maintenance costs. Currently, the unit holds meetings in rented facilities, and fitness classes at a senior center. Czech language classes are sponsored with the Czech Consulate General in Los Angeles. A popular Sokol Family Camp at Dinkey Creek has been in operation since 1969. The camp, which evolved from a children's camp, is now popular with several generations.

Sokols in Malin and Scio, Oregon. These two small Oregon towns, with populations less than 1,000, were settled mainly by Czechs. Jan Rosicky, a Czech immigrant publisher from Omaha helped found Malin, a farming town near the California border, where the earliest settlers were from Nebraska. The town was named after a town in Bohemia known for its radishes, because these vegetables were also plentiful in the Oregon settlement. The immigrants who settled in Malin faced many hardships associated with farming, but nevertheless started a school, Czech library, a ZCBJ Lodge, and a Sokol unit in 1909. Sokol Malin was strong during its early years, and hosted the Pacific District Slet in 1928. Scio, a town between Portland and Eugene, established a Sokol unit, Czech school, and a ZCBJ Lodge, with a Bohemian Hall, around 1911. The Czech school and Sokol organization were active until 1987.

Growth of the Sokol Units

At the onset of World War I, Sokol New York listed 525 members; the next two units with the most members were Chicago's *Plzeňsky* (Pilsen) and Chicago with 364 and 363, respectively. By 1925, Slávský in Cicero had 1,346 members and *Plzeňsky,* Chicago, and New York each listed about 800 members. Two more Sokols in Chicago, Havlíček-Tyrš and Town of Lake each had more than 500 members. Thus, five of the six Sokols with the most members were in Greater Chicago. During the period between World Wars, other units with high numbers of members were in cities with many Czech immigrants, i.e., Cleveland, Omaha, Baltimore, and St. Louis. Units in the Southern and Pacific Districts, established later, initially had fewer members. However, some units, e.g., Ft. Worth, Ennis, and Dallas, grew substantially.

In 1926, the Central District membership accounted for more than 50% of the total membership of ASO. A more impressive statistic is that about 40% of the adult ASO membership attended gymnastics/fitness classes in 1920s. The viability of Sokol units obviously required enough members for successful programs. Data from 1933 indicate that at least six units had fewer than twenty-five members, and not surprisingly did not survive after World War II, e.g., Manitowoc, Wisconsin, and Galveston.

Summary/Conclusions

As documented in this chapter, establishing Sokol units in the US was a task that required a vision supported by courage, determination, and sacrifice. The earliest units were established by the Czech immigrants themselves, with little, if any, help from businesses, government or large fund drives. Probably, the most impressive example of determination is that units rebuilt their halls after multiple fires, which were common for wooden buildings. Other units overcame financial problems, like those that occurred during the Great Depression, and were able to survive. Relationships with the German Turners were helpful in establishing the Sokol movement in the US, because 1) Sokols often used Turner facilities prior to owning their own, 2) Turner trainers were sometimes hired by Sokol units, and 3) a friendly competition exited between Sokol and Turner clubs. It is important to remember that the funds necessary to build and maintain Sokol halls were mostly from the members themselves, although fraternal and cultural organizations did provide some assistance. A key factor in the survival of the various Sokol units was their Czech identity and culture. As noted here, each gymnastic unit included, at least some, Czech cultural activity; very often theater/opera, or music groups. The inclusion of Czech theater is especially notable, even in very small towns. Czech neighborhoods were a key factor in establishing and maintaining Sokol units, because they served as fitness/cultural centers for youths and adults. Mergers of various clubs also increased their chances of survival.

5

Sokol's Contribution to Gymnastics in the US

Introduction

Gymnastics was introduced in the US during the early 19th century by the German Turnverein organization. With the establishment of Sokol clubs beginning in 1865, gymnastics enjoyed two major organizations promoting gymnastics as both a component of physical education and as a sport. The development of gymnastics in the US was facilitated by many members of these organizations. Moreover, the Turnverein and Sokol societies produced outstanding gymnasts of national and international caliber, as well as officials at all levels of the sport. Sokol influenced not only artistic gymnastics, but played a leadership role in the development of the relatively new sport of rhythmic gymnastics. Unfortunately, too often histories of Sokol clubs fail to cite this important contribution of the Sokol movement, and to recognize the members who brought Sokol gymnastics to a level of excellence. This chapter highlights the contributions of some of the Sokol members who brought recognition to the organization by excelling in the sport of gymnastics, and those members who promoted and supported the sport in a variety of ways.

History of Gymnastics

Greek origins. Literature from ancient Greece indicates that some 2,500 years ago there were sporting events in Athens that consisted of gymnastic activities, e.g., tumbling, and rope climbing. These activities were components of tournaments in Athens, where the gymnasium was the hub of activity. Greeks, like Tyrš centuries later, believed that symmetry between mind and body was possible only when physical exercise was coupled with intellectual activity. The term "artistic gymnastics" originated during the early 19th century to distinguish the free-flowing exercises from those used for military objectives.

International gymnastics in Europe. "At the time international gymnastics was being organized, gymnastics in Europe included a variety of current apparatuses and other activities such as: traveling rings, carousels, rope climb, the buck, wall ladders (also known as Swedish ladders), stunts, tumbling, pyramids, horizontal and vertical ladders" (Norma Zabka personal communication, 2018). The balance beam and uneven (asymmetric) bars were introduced as competitive events by the Germans and Czechs respectively. All gymnastic skills, i.e., strength, flexibility, balance, and agility, were represented in the events selected for competition. At the first modern Olympics in 1896, gymnastics was included and has remained in all subsequent Olympic Games. However, some gymnastic events, e.g., rope climbing and tumbling, have not survived, perhaps because they are not considered to be "artistic."

Gymnastics has philosophical roots. The term "gymnastics" in Greek culture was defined as exercise training in the nude, and thus was not identical to the modern definition of the term. Advocates of physical activity in the late 18th and early 19th centuries were Germans who recognized the mental and moral values of exercise regimens. For example, Johann Bernhard Basedow (1723–1790) was an early writer regarding the value of physical activity as a means of developing the mind and body (Zwarg, 1981). Similarly, Gerhard Vieth (1783–1836) wrote an encyclopedia of bodily exercise in which he emphasized the idea that the value of exercises should be regarded as mental and moral (Zwarg, 1981). These early advocates of physical training subscribed activities such as swinging, jumping, and vaulting; these terms suggest "types of gymnastics." The development of the events that we now recognize comprising gymnastics had their origins in Germany. Johann GutsMuths (1759–1839) taught physical education in Germany in 1784 and combined "exercises from Greek pentathlon, such as running, jumping, wrestling and throwing the discus and lance, with sports of burghers (prosperous citizens) and aristocratic training on specially adapted apparatus" (Nolte, 2002, 7–8). GutsMuths developed a system of physical exercise for the schools, which was widely implemented in Germany and other European countries. He wrote a seminal book on gymnastics for youth: *Gymnastik far die Jungend,* now available in English (Andesite Press, 2017); he is recognized as the "grandfather" of gymnastics (Goodbody, 1982, 12–13). During the early 1800s his system was popular and provided a foundation for the establishment of the German Turnverein by Fredrich Ludwig Jahn (1778–1852), who started the open-air gymnasium (Turnplatz) in 1811. His gymnasium included rings, parallel bars, balance beam, and horizontal bar, which are events included in today's artistic gymnastic competitions. Thus, Jahn is recognized as the father of gymnastics.

Other systems of gymnastics. Adolf Spiess introduced a system based on anatomical principles, which required a gymnast to "pass from one apparatus to another" (Maháček, 1938, 74). Its shortcoming was that only very small groups could be accommodated. Nevertheless, this system spread through gymnasiums in Switzerland, France, and Belgium. Jahn's peer, Peter Henry Ling, is recognized as the father of Swedish gymnastics; his system placed less emphasis on strength and included "free calisthenics" for four objectives: pedagogic, military, medical, and aesthetic (Brodin, 2008). The Swedish system utilized the beam, wall bars, window-ladder, and box (Goodbody, 1982). When Miroslav Tyrš developed the Sokol system in 1862, he utilized mostly Jahn's Turnverein training tools, but encouraged the use of elements of what are now known as "rhythmic gymnastics" (hoops, Indian clubs, ribbons, and balls). Jandisek and Pelikán (1952) noted that the first Indian club performance was by the American Sokols at Český Brod in 1887. Such exercise accessories were components of the gymnastics system that underscored the idea of aesthetic gymnastics, and inspired Catharine Beecher to teach a new form of dance-inspired exercise; she used Ling's ideas to create a "grace without dancing." Thus, both rhythmic and artistic modern gymnastics have roots dating back to the 19th century. Rhythmic gymnastics is discussed later in this chapter.

Artistic Gymnastics becomes an "organized international sport." During the late 19th century, gymnastics competitions were occurring in Europe, thus in 1881, the Bureau of the European Gymnastics Federation was formed, and later became the Fédération Inernationale de Gymnastique or International Gymnastics Federation (FIG). Men's gymnastics in the first modern Olympic Games, held in Athens in 1896, included: horizontal bar, parallel bars, pommel horse, rings and vault, as well as rope climb, high jump, and running. Gymnastics in the US, was first governed by the Amateur Athletic Union, beginning in 1883, but later (1963) a separate governing body limited to gymnastics, the US Gymnastics Federation, now USA Gymnastics, was established. Since 1956, the Olympic men's gymnastics events have included horizontal bar, parallel bars, pommel horse, vault, rings, and floor exercise. Women's events are floor exercise, uneven bars, vault, and balance beam.

United States gymnasts in the Olympics, 1920–1932. The first time US gymnasts competed in the Olympic Games was in 1920 (Antwerp); that team included Frank Kriz of Sokol New York. Four years later, three Sokols earned spots of the 1924 team: Frank Kriz (New York), Rudolf Novak (Cedar Rapids), and Frank Safanda (D.A. Sokol, New York). Kriz was selected for his third Olympic Games in 1928. Details of Sokols in the Olympics and World Championships are found in a subsequent section of this chapter.

Evolution of the Artistic Gymnastics Events

The six men's and four women's artistic gymnastics events have undergone significant changes over the last millennium. These changes include not only the performances themselves, but the apparatuses utilized. This section summarizes how these artistic gymnastics events have evolved. More detailed information regarding the changes in these events is found in Grossfeld (2014).

Pommel horse. A wooden horse that lacked pommels was used by soldiers to practice mounting and dismounting more than 2,000 years ago. Pommels were added in the 17th century, and Fredrich Ludwig Jahn included this apparatus in his Turnverein training program in the early 19th century. The long horse was designed with an elevated end (neck) and used for vaulting as well as a side horse (pommel horse) by adding the pommels. A full symmetrical version was finally introduced by Americans in 1948, and in 1980 the size of the pommels was increased to facilitate simultaneous multi-hand placements on one pommel. Then the width of the horse's body was increased in 2008.

The original dual-purpose horse used as pommel horse, and for vaulting after the removal of the pommels.

Vaulting table. As noted above the horse was utilized for vaulting for a very long time; men vaulted over the length of the horse, whereas women vaulted over its side. The horse was not an ideal apparatus for vaulting, especially for men, because the width of the apparatus was too narrow to accommodate men's shoulder width. Not until the year 2000 was the horse replaced by a table. Following the submission of six versions of the vaulting table, two models were approved for international competitions.

Rings. Originally swinging (flying) rings were used in schools. During the first decade of the 20th century there was no consensus regarding the use of still or swinging rings in gymnastics competitions. Even in the 1920s, swinging (steel) rings were frequently used in German competitions. Rings made of wood replaced those forged of metal. Surprisingly, flying (swinging) rings continued to be an event in US high schools and colleges until the mid-1950s.

Balance beam. "Rails" were the precursors of the beam and were utilized by soldiers to develop balance. In Jahn's outdoor gymnasium, in 1814, they were also used for climbing (Frederick, 1984). The flat-surface beam then replaced the rail, and finally in 1934 the balance beam was included in international gymnastic competitions. Acrobatic skills on the beam were introduced in the 1960s, and in 1980 a spring reflex mechanism was added to the beam's aluminum core, in order to cushion some of the skills requiring landing on the beam.

Parallel bars/uneven bars. Jahn's Turnverein employed parallel bars to train gymnasts for the pommel horse. Most of the skills were power exercises employed to increase strength, but competition on the parallel bars was included in the first modern Olympics in 1896. A major problem with the use of parallel bars in competitions was that they were not standardized, i.e., some were flexible, others were somewhat rigid. It was not until the 1950s that norms were prescribed and led to the production of bars that do not lose their stability, despite heavy use. In 1963, fiber glass parallel bar rails were introduced because they were safer than wood, which if broken could injure the performer. Uneven bars (asymmetric parallel bars) for women was a variation of parallel bars, with one bar higher than the other. Although introduced in the 1930s by the Czech Sokols, it did not become an Olympic event until 1952.

Horizontal bar. As far back as ancient Greece and Rome and into the middle-ages the horizontal bar was used by acrobats (Butterworth, 1902). GutsMuths, Jahn's predecessor, introduced this apparatus to gymnasts in 1793, and Jahn utilized the apparatus in the Turnverein movement and developed its use (Goodbody, 1982, 11–18). The horizontal bar was already an event in the 1896 Olympic Games, but underwent variations in construction. Some horizontal bars were wood, and the diameter of the bar was variable. An increase in the width of the bar from seven to eight feet has resulted in a greater elasticity of the bar.

Floor (Free) exercise. Acrobatic routines on the floor were commonly used many centuries ago by traveling groups of dancers and tumblers. But it was the Swede, Ling, who was the primary teacher of "natural gymnastics" (performances without the use of any apparatus) during the early 19th century. This system of exercise, with the addition of tumbling, evolved into the gymnastic event known as "floor exercise." A proposal that free exercises be included in world competition was made in 1923 and led to the event's inclusion in the 1930 World Championships. The area of the floor was increased in 1952, and as more difficult tumbling skills were being utilized, springs were added to the floor in 1979.

Trampoline and tumbling. These two events are not included in the all-around competitions for men or women and lie outside the category of "artistic gymnastics." However, they each have important histories and continue to have an impact on the sport. Tumbling is, of course, centuries old and has been a source of entertainment in many societies. Trampoline, as we know it today, was developed by George Nissen, a University of Iowa gymnast, in 1936. He heard "el trampolin" while he was in Mexico then added "e" to the word and began manufacturing the apparatus in 1942. He developed an international trampoline market. Trampolines have served several purposes, including astronaut training and the development of gymnastic skills. Competition on the trampoline was common in high schools, colleges, and clubs, but was discontinued for a long period of time, because of the many serious injuries and the resulting lawsuits. However, in 1964, the event became an international sport and was added as an Olympic sport in 2000. Tumbling, has a similar history, i.e., was a component of high school and college gymnastics until the late 1960s. It was an event in the World Championships in the 1880s and only once (1932) in the Olympics. In 2011, the College Sport of Acrobatics and Tumbling became a reality. Two years later USA Gymnastics added Team Acrobatics and Tumbling as a sport for youths. The use of tumbling and trampoline in training for artistic gymnastics remain valuable tools for learning new skills.

Organizations and Pioneers of USA Gymnastics

This topic, covered in detail by Grossfeld (2010), is briefly summarized here. It was the disciples of Fredrich Ludwig Jahn, the father of the Turnverein movement in Germany, who are credited with introducing gymnastics in the US in the 1820s. The first two universities to include the Turnverein system of gymnastics were Harvard and Yale, and in 1848 the first Turnverein club was established in Cincinnati. As German immigrants settled, the Turnverein movement grew, so that by 1894 there were 317 clubs in the US. Many Swiss Turnvereins were also established. YMCA (Young Mens Christian Association), as early as 1868, equipped their gymnasiums with gymnastics apparatuses, thereby introducing its members to gymnastic training and the sport of gymnastics. The training of physical education instructors for the YMCA's was provided by Springfield College in Massachusetts, and facilitated the development of some outstanding gymnasts developed by the YMCA. Due to the availability of competent coaches, the sport underwent a revival in the early 1920s in Eastern colleges, namely MIT, Princeton, Dartmouth, and the Naval Academy

(Comiskey, 1983, S–25). The proliferation of Sokol clubs, beginning with the formation of Sokol St. Louis in 1865, also played a major role in establishing gymnastics in the USA. These clubs, founded by Czech, Slovak, and Polish (Falcons) immigrants, trained gymnasts and promoted the sport of gymnastics. Thus, the development of gymnastics in the US is truly a gift from European immigrants.

Prominent Sokols in the Development of Gymnastics

Marie Provazníková. Born Marie Kalous in 1890 in Bohemia, her lifetime of one hundred years was filled with leadership, courage, and dedication to both gymnastics and physical education. As Director of Women in her Czech homeland, she had a profound influence on gymnastics in the Sokol organization. Moreover, she was a founding member of the Fédération Inernationale de Gymnastique (FIG), and served as Chair of the Women's Technical Committee. Her influence on gymnastics and physical education was also facilitated by her many other roles, including serving on the advisory committee of the Ministry of Public Health as head of the Department of Girl's and Women's Physical Education. As detailed in Dusek's Ph.D. thesis (1981), Provazníková was viewed as a dynamic and innovative teacher, and was instrumental in advancing girl's and women's gymnastics, and physical education to the highest levels. In Prague's Charles University she was a Professor who developed women's programs and trained teachers of physical education. With the formation of FIG, in 1920, she helped lay the foundation for, and held various positions on the Women's Technical Committee. She wrote many papers and books on gymnastics and physical education. One of her lasting contributions was her role in developing the uneven (high/low) bars for women's competition and modifying the balance beam as competitive events. She is also remembered for directing the women's events in the 1932 and 1938 Slets. Marie Provazníková was the chief organizer of the 1948 Women's Olympic Gymnastics Competition in London. The Czech Women's team, which she led, won the team gold medal in that Olympiad. As noted in Chapter 2, Provazníková could not return to her homeland, knowing that she would be arrested because of her resistance to the Communist government. She then came to the US, where she spent the rest of her life.

Provazníková taught at the Panzer College of Physical Education in East Orange, New Jersey, and became a member of Sokol New York. She was asked to create a rhythmic gymnastics number for the US women's Olympic team in 1952 and served on the President's Council on Physical Fitness. Her contributions to Sokol are varied and impressive. She formed the "Czechoslovak Sokols Abroad" organization and directed and promoted camps for Sokols in Austria, France, and Switzerland; moreover, she was a member of the organization committees for Slets in those countries, as well as in the US and Canada. Provazníková was a prolific writer and is credited with numerous books on gymnastics terminology; she revised manuals and served as a consultant for gymnastics organizations. Her last book, *To Byl Sokol (That was Sokol)* recalls the Sokol movement and its contributions. Her outstanding lifetime work and leadership has been recognized by the numerous awards she has received. These include French Legion d'Honeur, Yugoslavia's Sava Cravette, the Order of Tomáš Garigue Masaryk, and the key to the City of Chicago.

Jarka Jelinek (1892–1962). Jelinek was an outstanding gymnast and coach in Bohemia. He helped establish Sokol clubs in Russia and then in Slovakia, and in 1921 he immigrated to the US, where he remained. His work with the American Sokol Organization is legendary: he trained many gymnasts, composed compulsory gymnastics routines and mass drills, taught in instructor's courses, edited the technical section of the Sokol American publication, and organized five national Slets. Jelinek trained many outstanding gymnasts.

Mildred Prchal (1895–1983). She was called "Great Lady," and certainly earned the title. Born Mildred Prochaska in Chicago she began her gymnastics training five years later at Sokol Pilsen and then at Havliček-Tyrš. Her talents included ballet, acrobatics, and tap dance, as well gymnastics, which she taught. In 1920, as a member of the American Sokol Organization gymnastic team competing in Prague at the VII Slet, she extended her European visit to attend schools in Prague in rhythmics and fencing, and then studied classical ballet and acrobatics in Paris. Subsequently, she opened a ballet school in Berwyn, Illinois, where one of her students, John Kriza, went on to a long career as a professional dancer with the American Ballet Theatre. Mildred Prchal is remembered for her compositions of rhythmic and artistic gymnastic performances. Her support for women in gymnastics was evident early in her career. After she organized the first Women's Instructors Board at Sokol Havliček-Tyrš in 1920, she urged the American Sokol Organization to give women leadership roles for all female activities, which they did in 1921, and two years later a Women's Board of Instructors was established. She wrote, illustrated, and published *Artistic Gymnastics—Floor Exercises for Women,* as well as three books on rhythmic exercises and many articles for Sokol and other publications. Thus, Mildred Prchal is recognized for her many contributions to both artistic and rhythmic gymnastics. She was a pioneer in the development of rhythmic gymnastics in the US, and arranged the first national championships in 1973.

Mildred Prchal received many honors, including induction into the prestigious United States Gymnastics Hall of Fame, and as recipient of the United States Gymnastics Federation's Master of Sports Award. She is also listed in *Who's Who in Gymnastics,* and *Who's Who in American Women.* Her contributions spanned Sokol and the national and international spheres of gymnastics. She taught in many Sokol instructor's schools, was National Director of Women for ASO from 1953–1965, served on the Olympic Committee, and chaired the United States Gymnastics Federation Rhythmic Gymnastics Committee. Mildred was married to Charles Prchal who served as president of the ASO from 1943 until 1965. Her legacy includes contributions to artistic and rhythmic gymnastics, dance, women's roles in Sokol, and inspiring young people. She died in 1983 and continues to be remembered as "Great Lady."

Norma Zabka. This Sokol New York lifetime member, was born across the street from her Sokol gym and was an outstanding artistic gymnast winning the gold medal in the Junior National Amateur Athletic Union Championship, as well as the National American Sokol Championship in 1948. Zabka taught at Hunter College in New York City and attended the Sokol Berryville Camp for Rhythmic Gymnastics

Trainers, a sport that was new in the US. This led to her pioneering work in the new sport and earned her a place in the US Gymnastics Hall of Fame where she was recognized for her service as a national and international judge. Her judging experiences include some thirty-two international championships (Olympic, World, Pan American, and National). She was a charter member and chairperson of USA Rhythmic Gymnastics, and has authored numerous gymnastic articles, including *Gymnastic Activities with Hand Apparatus for Girls and Boys,* a book co-authored with Marie Provazníková. Her contributions also include chairing the Pan American Rhythmic Gymnastics Committee and the USGA Rhythmic Gymnastics Committee. She is also known for her lifetime service and leadership in the American Sokol Organization including teaching at many instructor's schools, and her work in making Sokol New York a leader in the Sokol movement.

Stanley Barcal (1912–2003). An American Sokol National Junior Champion in 1929 and Senior Champion in 1947, Stan Barcal continued to promote gymnastics and the Sokol movement throughout his life. He competed for the ASO in the 1932 and 1938 Slets in Prague and taught gymnastics at three Sokol units: Rozvoj, Chicago, and Berwyn. Barcal served Sokol Chicago as Director of Men (nineteen years) and president (thirty-one years), and the ASO as a member of the Board of Instructors (forty-six years). Stan Barcal was a consistent contributor to the sport of gymnastics for at least sixty years. He developed compulsory routines for competitions, preserved the history of ASO, with a focus on gymnastic training and competitions. It is his unwavering recognition that gymnastics is the core of the Sokol movement that underscores Stan Barcal's enduring contribution to gymnastics.

Henry Smidl (1894–1985). A competitor for Sokol Chicago, Smidl won numerous Sokol national and international gold medals between 1916 and 1927. His role in introducing, promoting, and coaching high school gymnastics in Illinois earned him induction into the US Gymnastics Hall of Fame in 1960. While teaching at Englewood High School in Chicago he developed an intramural gymnastics program, then inspired the staffs at Harrison High and Lane Tech to form teams, which was the beginning of high school competitive gymnastics in Illinois. Smidl also coached gymnastics at Sokol Chicago and later at Lindblom High School, where he developed a gymnastics dynasty. Like the Sokols, Illinois high schools offered three levels of gymnastics competitions and Smidl devoted his time evenly between the three skill levels. Accordingly, his championships far exceeded those won by other coaches. He was admired for his work in developing the sport in Illinois high schools, and for inspiring gymnasts and coaches during his twenty-five years of service. In 1957, he was named "Outstanding Coach" by the American Athletic Association.

Jerry Hardy. A Sokol New York member, and outstanding gymnast, Hardy was inducted into National Judges Hall of Fame in 1982 and into the US Gymnastics Hall of Fame in 1989. His contributions to the sport of gymnastics, included representing Sokol New York on the New York AAU Board for nearly three decades and then serving on the National AAU Board for ten years. He was the Head Coach of the US. Pan American Team (1955), and US Team Manager at the Moscow World Championships (1958). Hardy's legacy is his contributions to national and international artistic gymnastics judging, and his promotion of the sport.

Jerry Milan. Few Sokol members have served the organization and gymnastics in the variety of ways that Jerry Milan has. He coached in high schools and Sokol, and trained many gymnastic instructors. Moreover he served as president and physical director of Sokol Fort Worth. His interest in gymnastics has underscored his many contributions to the sport. Jerry and his wife Henrietta (nee Banfi), a 1959 Sokol champion, and their sons Rome and Talon have attended all Olympic Games from 1968 to 2016, and Jerry has served on the US Olympic Committee (1972), and Pan American Games Committee (1971), and the United States Gymnastics Federation Board. He has also directed gymnastics championship meets, e.g., American Sokol, Texas High School, and World Gymnastics Championships. He and his son Rome have promoted gymnastics and Sokol in a variety of ways. Rome's traveling Sokol exhibit, which documents the evolution and gymnastics and the history of Sokol, has reached many people. Jerry's service on national and international committees has brought recognition to Sokol's contributions to a broader community. He is the recipient of many service awards, including the Gymnastic Association of Texas, and the United States Gymnastic Federation; in 2013 he was inducted into the Texas

Stan Barcal, Sokol Chicago
(Photo American Sokol Organization)

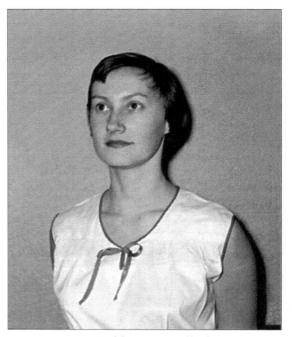

Norma Zabka, US Hall of Fame
honoree from Sokol New York

Mildred Prchal, US Hall of Fame honoree from Sokol Tabor at the 1955 Sokol instructor's course in St. Louis.

*Jerry and Henrietta Milan,
Sokol Fort Worth*

*Ellen Nyemcsik, a US Gymnastics Hall of Fame honoree,
from Sokol Little Ferry demonstrates the use of a ribbon,
a hand apparatus used in rhythmic gymnastics.*

High School Gymnastics Coaches Hall of Honor.

Emil Milan (1929–2016), Jerry's brother, also a member of Sokol Fort Worth, was a dedicated visionary who is recognized as the "Father of Texas High School Gymnastics." It was Emil Milan, following his coaching at Sokol Fort Worth, who founded high school gymnastics in his state. His Bell High School boys' teams won fourteen state titles, his girls teams won three state titles, and many of his athletes earned All-American honors. He was honored four times as National High School Gymnastics Coach of the Year, and in 1993 he was selected as the National Association of College Gymnastics Coaches Honor Coach. Emil Milan was also a member of the US Olympic Women's Gymnastics Committee from 1966–1969. He coordinated the International Invitation Gymnastics Meet and American Cup from 1980–1982, and hosted the first National High School Gymnastics Championships in 1988.

Ellen Garlicki Nyemcsik. A member of Sokol Little Ferry, Nyemcsik introduced rhythmic gymnastics to her region, where she served as the Administrative Chairperson in the late 1970s and the early 1980s. Her contributions include teaching gymnastics to both gymnasts and physical educators in summer camps. While she served on the National Technical Committee, Nyemcsik established judging rules for the US Rhythmic Gymnastics Competitive Program and was appointed Master Judge Clinician. Her contributions to the sport of rhythmic gymnastics have spanned all levels: competitor, coach, administrator, and judge. She trained as an artistic gymnast and competed in high school and college. In 1971, she switched to rhythmic gymnastics and went on to compete in the 1978 Pan Pacific Championships, and the 1979 World Championships. Nyemcsik was the first organizer and chairperson of USA Rhythmic Gymnastics Region 5, while she was active in the sport as a competitor, coach, and judge. Her many contributions have been recognized by USA Gymnastics, an organization that honored her for her more than twenty years of service in 2000, and then, in 2010, by induction into the US Gymnastics Hall of Fame. Ellen Nyemcsik is still active in judging and assigns judges to competitions.

International Sokol Champions and Competitors

Sokol clubs in the United States have developed many good male and female gymnasts, some of whom have attained international status. Many have competed on high school and college teams, and in national meets, e.g. AAU, USA Gymnastics. This section is limited to those Sokol-trained gymnasts that were members of US International or Olympic gymnastics teams or won a US national title.

First half of the 20th Century

Frank Jirasek. The first US Sokol gymnast of fame was Frank Jirasek from New York and then Cedar Rapids. He was a two-time all-around National AAU Gymnastics Champion (1909 and 1910), and he also won gold medals on the parallel bars in both of those years. In 1909, he represented Sokol New York and in 1910, Sokol Tyrš—Cedar Rapids, where he became that unit's instructor. The high caliber of Sokol gymnasts during the early 20th century is evidenced by the facts that Sokol New York (Bohemian Gymnastic Association) won the team title in 1910, and their team member, William Heisler, placed second behind Jirasek in the all-around event, and won gold medals in the long horse vault in 1909 and 1910. Jirasek helped the Sokols in Ennis, Texas, form their gymnastics program, and then in 1914 he became the Physical Director of Sokol Pilsen in Chicago.

Frank Kriz (1894–1955). Son of Czech immigrants and a member of Sokol New York, Kriz was a legendary Sokol gymnast, as indicated by his long career in international and national competitions. He began competing in gymnastics in 1908, when he was fourteen years of age, and in addition to winning many medals in Sokol competitions, Kriz won seven National AAU titles during his twenty-two-year career, including the coveted all-around gold medal in 1922 and 1924. Moreover, he also won the vault in 1918 and 1922, parallel bars in 1922, and floor exercise in 1924. Kris was a member of three Olympic teams, including the first US team to compete in an overseas Olympics, which was held in Antwerp in 1920. He distinguished himself as the 10th best all-around gymnast in the world in that Olympiad. In the 1924 Olympic Games, held in Paris, Kriz won the gold medal on the vault event, which in that Olympic competition required the gymnast to clear a high jump bar prior to finishing the vault on the long horse. The silver and bronze medals in that event were won by Czech Sokols. Kriz continued his gymnastics career and was selected for the 1928 Olympic team. He was the top US gymnast on the 1920 and 1924 Olympic teams, and in 1928, at the

age of thirty-four he earned the third best score of the US team. Kriz, a New York City firefighter, demonstrated his commitment to gymnastics training when he erected a horizontal bar behind his firehouse for additional training. Frank Kriz was inducted posthumously into the US Gymnastics Hall of Fame in 1959 and is recognized as the first American Olympian to win a medal in a gymnastics competition held outside the US. He was unquestionably the best American gymnast during the decade following World War I.

Rudolf Novak (1889–1968). Another Sokol, selected for the 1924 US Olympic gymnastics team was Rudolf Novak of Cedar Rapids, who was thirty-five years of age at the time. Novak was an immigrant from Bohemia, and became an accomplished gymnast during his teen years, and then enrolled in Michigan's Olivet College where he played football, before resuming his gymnastics training at Sokol Cedar Rapids.

Frank Safanda (1895–1948). The third Sokol member of the US 1924 men's Olympic Gymnastics Team was Frank Safanda, a machinist who lived in New Jersey and was a member of New York City D.A. Sokol.

Rudolf Hradecky (1909–1993). The Czech-born Hradecky immigrated, at the age of one, with his parents to New York and joined Sokol there as a teenager. He was a multi-sport athlete, but his ability in the vault (long horse) was exceptional, as he won the National AAU championship in 1928 at the age of nineteen. He enjoyed a long, nineteen-year career, subsequently winning gold medals in the vault event at the National AAU Championships in 1936, 1944, 1946, and 1947. Hradecky is a US Gymnastics Hall of Fame honoree. His victories in the vault are especially impressive because he won the titles competing against many other future Hall of Famers and Olympic team members. He was Sokol New York's Director of Men during World War II and was an inspiration for gymnasts who wanted to excel in the sport. He died in 1993. Norma Zabka wrote: "Sokol New York was fortunate to have Bro. Hradecky serve as Director of Men during World War II. He served as an exemplary role model, particularly for junior gymnasts, and he fondly recalled working with excellent gymnasts such as Jerry Hardy," also a Gymnastics Hall of Fame Honoree.

Paul Fina (1916–2009). Sokol Chicago's Paul Fina was an outstanding gymnast who won the NCAA all-around title in 1940 and again in 1941, competing for the University of Illinois. Following his collegiate career, he won the National AAU floor exercise gold medal in 1946 and was a member of the US International Gymnastics team in 1947. Although Fina was selected as a member of the 1940 US Olympic Gymnastics Team, the Olympics were cancelled because of World War II. His interest in gymnastics continued for many later decades, as evidenced by his membership on the Olympic Gymnastics Committee (1968, 1972), his service as an International Judge, and as an ASO representative on the US Gymnastic Federation Council. He also was one of the major organizers of the United States Gymnastics Federation and served on the ASO Board for twenty years. Fina was inducted into the US Gymnastics Hall of Fame in 1970 and is remembered as an enthusiastic supporter of gymnastics and the Sokol movement.

Ladislava (Laddie) Bakanic. A life-long New York Sokol member, Laddie Bakanic was a 1948 US Women's Gymnastics Team member. Her team placed third, the first time the US women's gymnastics team medaled in the Olympic Games. The team gold medal was won by the Czech Sokol team. In a 2016 interview with the *Wall Street Journal,* the ninety-two-year-old Bakanic recalled how she trained at the Sokol gym after work, alongside men, including her husband, on four or five days per week. For her "gymnastics was something I loved to do." Bakanic, born in 1924 (nee Hniz), was coached by her father, who was President of Sokol New York, when she was a child. Her talents were recognized as she won most Sokol meets as a junior girl, and in 1941 became the AAU Junior Champion. In 1944, Bakanic placed second in the Senior AAU Championships and met her future husband when he came to Sokol New York to train. She planned on attending the 1948 Sokol Slet in Prague, but her father suggested that she tryout for the US Women's Olympic Gymnastics Team, and to her surprise she made the team. After the Olympics, she retired from competitive gymnastics and raised a family. Bakanic is the only surviving member of the 1948 gymnastics team.

Last Half of the 20th Century

James (Jim) Hartung. A USA Hall of Fame gymnast, Hartung began training at a very early age at Sokol Omaha, under the guidance of Phil Cahoy Sr.

The coach's son, Phil Jr. was also training there, and the two young gymnasts demonstrated that they each had promising futures. Hartung became a state high school champion, leading his team to four consecutive state championships and earning eighteen gold medals. His high school coach at Omaha South High was Richard Beran, also a member of Sokol Omaha. In 1978 Hartung was selected as the athlete of the year by the *Omaha World Herald* newspaper and went on to excel in gymnastics at the University of Nebraska. He set NCAA records for individual event championships (seven) and gold medals (eleven). Hartung proved to be the best collegiate gymnast by the time he was a junior at the University of Nebraska by winning the NCAA all-around gold medal; during his collegiate career he won twenty-two All-American Awards. He earned a spot on the 1980 US Olympic team, but because the Soviet Union invaded Afghanistan, the US boycotted the 1980 Olympic Games and he did not participate. Four years later, Hartung was a member of the US Men's Olympic team that won the gold medal. He also was a member of four US International gymnastics teams (1978, 1979, 1981, and 1983). Hartung credits Sokol Omaha's Phil Cahoy Sr., as the most influential coach who trained him (for twelve years).

Phil Cahoy Jr. Like Jim Hartung, Phil Cahoy Jr. began gymnastic training with his father (Phil Sr.) at Sokol Omaha when he first started elementary school, and like Hartung, became an NCAA gold medalist. The two aspiring gymnasts became good friends. Phil Cahoy Jr. was also a member of Omaha South High's three-year run of state championships, and in 1978 he placed first in six gymnastics events. He then won the NCAA national championship competing for the University of Nebraska. A 2001 inductee of the USA Gymnastics Hall of Fame, Phil Cahoy was a member of four World Championship teams. His six-foot-one- inch frame is unusual in the gymnastics world, since competitors are usually several inches shorter than that. He is currently an orthopedic surgeon in Grand Island, Nebraska. Another outstanding gymnast, Chuck Chmelka, currently the head gymnastics coach at the University of Nebraska Lincoln, also trained under Phil Cahoy Sr. during his youth. Moreover, like Hartung and Cahoy Jr., he was also on the South High team that was coached by Richard Beran, who also trained at Sokol Omaha.

Both photos courtesy of *Lincoln Star Journal*

At right: *Phil Cahoy Jr., US Olympian and US Hall of Fame honoree from Sokol Omaha*

Below: *James Hartung, US Olympian and US Hall of Fame honoree from Sokol Omaha*

Mike Wilson. This gymnast began his training as a youngster, along with his sister at Sokol Dallas under Walter Hosek and Bill Willis. His Sokol training provided him with the skills necessary for high school competitive gymnastics. He then excelled in the sport at Garland High School. His skills earned him a scholarship at the University of Oklahoma, where he competed from 1975 to 1979 and contributed to several of his university's National NCAA Championships. Wilson earned a place on the 1980 US Olympic team, along with Sokol Omaha's Phil Cahoy Jr. and James Hartung, but also missed his opportunity to compete because of the US boycott of the games. Mike Wilson then excelled in building charities and nonprofits, and is recognized as a philanthropist.

Rhythmic Gymnastics Becomes a Sport

Birth of rhythmic gymnastics. As reported by Ellen Nyemcsik (personal communication), rules for a new sport initially called "Modern Gymnastics" were developed in the early 1950s, and then in 1963 a Rhythmic Gymnastics World Championship competition was hosted in Europe, where the sport was very popular. Routines consisted of a dance with pre-acrobatic movements performed with hand apparatus (ball, hoops, clubs, ribbon, or rope). Sokol's Mildred Prchal, who was a member of the United States Gymnastics Federation, was asked by Frank Bare, the president of that governing body, to attend the World Championships in Bulgaria and organize the sport in the US. Prchal then contacted Sokol members and organized the first Rhythmic Gymnastics summer school in Berryville, New York. She then recruited teachers for the camp who understood the use of the various hand-held apparatus required for rhythmic gymnastics. Two other Sokols, Maria Provazníková and Norma Zabka, had written a book on the use of hand-held apparatus, and Zabka joined Mildred Prchal as an instructor at the camp.

Essence of the sport. Rhythmic gymnastics evolved as an international sport, with World Championships held biannually since 1963. In 1984, the sport became an individual Olympic event, and group competition (six gymnasts) was added in 1996. Rhythmic gymnastics continues requiring manipulation of an apparatus (balls, ribbons, clubs, ropes, or hoops) while performing a dance-like routine to music, that involves leaps, contortions, and flexibility. Such routines require hand-eye coordination, body coordination, agility, strength, and a keen ear for music. The sport is, in some ways, like ice-dancing. Individual competitions require routines performed for sixty to ninety seconds. Synchronized group routines are of 150–180 seconds in duration. Training for rhythmic gymnastics is intense and exhausting, and includes exercises for strength, flexibility, coordination, and dance. "The sport offers total physical exercise, grace and beauty of movement, creativity, and self-expression. It teaches appreciation of an art of physical movement and provides enjoyment of aesthetic satisfaction" (Schmidt, 1984, 71).

History of the sport. Andrea Schmidt (1984), who was the director of the United States Gymnastics Federation Rhythmic Gymnastics Committee, summarized the history of this new sport. Initially, group rhythmic gymnastics was a component of artistic gymnastics, with the women also competing on the four artistic events. However, the International Gymnastics Federation (FIG) excluded group rhythmic gymnastics after the 1956 Olympic Games. Nevertheless, rhythmic gymnastics was becoming popular, especially in Eastern European countries. Thus, in 1962, it was recognized as an independent women's sport by the FIG. Since 1963, World Rhythmic Gymnastics competitions have been held every two years. Finally, in 1984, the sport was added to the Olympic Games. American Sokol's Mildred Prchal was instrumental in gaining the acceptance of rhythmic gymnastics to the United States Gymnastics Federation program in 1969. As noted in the previous section (Prominent Sokols in the development of gymnastics), both Norma Zabka (Sokol New York) and Ellen Garlicki Nyemcsik (Sokol Little Ferry, NJ) are also pioneers in the sport of rhythmic gymnastics and inductees in the United States Gymnastics Hall of Fame. Sokol New York's Norma Zabka has been a pioneer in the development and progress of the sport, by her contribution as a judge in national and international competitions, and her numerous articles. Ellen Garlicki Nyemcsik of Sokol Little Ferry, New Jersey, has been involved in all aspects of the sport since its inception and has been instrumental in the growth and organization of the sport in the USA. Both women have continued contributing to the sport into the 21st century.

Summary/Conclusions

Often overlooked is the well-documented fact that Sokol has played a major role in competitive gymnastics, not only Europe, but also in North America. While "gymnastics for all" was a cornerstone for the Sokol movement, gymnastics training in this organization also produced champions. In the Czech lands, Sokol was virtually the sole force that enabled the training of gymnastic champions. Czech and Czechoslovak international gymnastics teams were Sokol teams. Although that was not true in the US, Sokol still played a major role in the promotion and facilitation of the sport and trained many elite gymnasts. As noted in this chapter, the United States Gymnastic Federation has honored ten Sokol members in their Hall of Fame (four from Sokol New York, two from Sokol Omaha, and Sokol Chicago, and one each from Sokols Tabor, and Little Ferry). Moreover, eight Sokol-trained gymnasts have been members of US Olympic teams, and many have won US national titles. Sokol members have been very active in the sport as judges, coaches, meet organizers, and facilitators. They have served on the boards of the USA Gymnastics Federation, the US Olympic Committee, and several are recognized as founders of rhythmic gymnastics. Gymnastics as a basis of physical education and as a sport in the US was primarily a contribution of German and Czech immigrants who established Turner and Sokol clubs in their new homeland.

One of the major impediments in many Sokol units was the misunderstanding of the Sokol mantra: "neither profit nor glory." This mantra was intended to underscore that the volunteer work by Sokol members was for the good of the organization and not for their glory nor for financial renumeration. This was not intended to discourage gymnasts from becoming champions in their sport. Unfortunately, too often members and/or their units failed to recognize the achievements of their gymnasts. This misinterpretation was also used to prevent hiring "professional" gymnastics instructors. Another impediment against encouraging high level gymnastic performance was the idea

that Sokol's mission was primarily physical education and not high-level achievement. In fact, Tyrš was a proponent of gymnasts working together and encouraging each other, while trying to excel in a friendly competition. Thus, the misunderstood mantra deprived many talented gymnasts from fulfilling their potentials. Moreover, students of gymnastics may have discontinued gymnastics classes if they were discouraged by a lack of progress.

Rhythmic gymnasts with ribbons, clubs, hoop and ball (rope, the 5th apparatus is not shown).

90—

6
Sokol in the 21st Century

Introduction

The decline in Sokol membership and activity, beginning in the last two decades of the 20th century, and continuing to the present, is undeniable. Riha (1989, 9) notes that a 21.3% decline in American Sokol Organization membership occurred between 1980 and 1989, and he examines some factors that have contributed to the decline, e.g., loss of the Czech language and customs, and near disappearance of ethnic neighborhoods. Although the role of the Sokol movement as a call for physical fitness is readily appreciated, its call for brotherhood, a Czech nation, and democracy are much less known and appreciated with each successive generation. How can we expect our youth to identify with the sense of nationalism and struggles of an ethnic identity when they are so many generations removed from their ancestors? However, these are not the most critical factors underlying the decline of Sokol as a physical fitness organization. We have only to look at some units that have survived and even progressed, to see that Sokol programs can contribute to American life. This chapter considers the changes that have occurred over the last four decades, and even earlier, that have affected the Sokol programs.

The Czech Culture and American Life

Post-World War I Era (1920–1940)

Considering the great numbers of immigrants that arrived between 1890 and 1910, it is likely that the children of these immigrants were fluent in, or at least had adequate understanding of, the Czech language and customs. They were most likely raised in Czech communities and were fully exposed to the culture their parents treasured, which often included Sokol. They learned some history about the land of their parents, and if they joined Sokol, they learned what the Sokol movement entailed. The creation of Czechoslovakia (1918) occurred during their lifetime, or shortly before they were born, thus the founding of that nation was recent history. Sokol during these years was firmly entrenched in the Tyrš philosophy, and the various units were harmonious in their presentations of this system of gymnastics. The number of Sokol units in the US peaked in 1933 (see Appendix C), with ninety-eight units with either men, and/or men and women members, and another twenty units consisting of women. The units were in Czech neighborhoods in the cities, and in small towns with a high percentage of Czechs.

In summary, this era was characterized by a culture that was profoundly Czech, a fact that placed the Sokol movement in an environment that reflected the experiences and values of the immigrants who came from Bohemia and Moravia. Accordingly, Sokol was a success because of the environment in which it existed, and because of the importance that the immigrants and/or their children placed on the values of Sokol training and philosophy.

The 1940s and 1950s

This era was characterized by an increase in the relocation of American-Czechs from their settlements, especially after World War II. Nevertheless, Sokol continued to be relatively strong. As seen in Appendix D, there was a decline in the number of units by 1961, however many of the units that closed were in small towns. The reduction in the number of units in the cities was primarily a consequence of unit mergers. Most youth and adult members of Sokol were of Czech ancestry, a factor that helped maintain the traditions of their ancestors. These participants often were children, grandchildren, or great grandchildren of Czech immigrants. As noted in Table 5, there were about 4,000 participants in the VI ASO Slet in Chicago in 1941, the highest number of any US Slet. The 1947 Slet had 1,828 Sokols participating; the lower number, compared to the 1941 Slet, is primarily due to effects of the war years. The total number of gymnasts participating in the next two post-war Slets (1953 and 1957) was 1,270 and 1,528 respectively. Of special interest is that the percentage of those totals that competed in gymnastics was much higher, i.e., 71% and 70% respectively, than in the 37% and 27% that competed in the 1937 and 1941 Slets. These data reveal that the number of Sokols who marched onto the field and performed calisthenics and also competed in gymnastics increased significantly during the 1950s.

The 1960s and 1970s

Five Slets were held during these decades, with the total number of participants over 2,000 in 1961 and 1965, and 1,748 in 1969 (Table 5). However, during the 1960s the number of Slet participants competing in gymnastics was only 57, 56, and 39%, far fewer than that of the 1950s. The two Slets held in the 1970s hosted about the same number of gymnasts on the field and about the same percentage of those who competed in gymnastics, i.e., about half. One of the biggest changes during these two decades was that the junior competitors began to outnumber the seniors to the extent that they constituted 79 and 78% in the 1969 and 1973 Slets. Thus, these data reveal that the number of gymnasts competing in the Slets of the 1960s and 1970s decreased when compared to the Slets held in the 1950s, and that this decline can be contributed to fewer adult competitors. Although the number of women competing in the first three ASO Slets, held in the 1920s, was less than the number of men competing, the number of women competitors in the 1933 Slet and all subsequent Slets exceeded the number of men participating. Thus, over the years, the number of women and juniors competing in gymnastics increased, whereas the number of men competing decreased.

The 1980s and 1990s

In 1961, the ASO consisted of fifty-one clubs, with seventeen having separate men's and women's units, a number which declined by 1994, and then declined again by 2008 (Appendices D, E, and F). However, the total number of participants in the Slets up to the end of the 20th century was never lower than one thousand (Table 5). Rhythmic gymnastics competition was inaugurated at the 1977 Slet and continued to be an event during the next nine Slets.

The 21st Century

The largest decline in Slet participation has occurred during the 21st century, as evidenced by the fact that the average participation in the five Slets held between 2001 and 2017 was 718. Considering the decline in the number of active Sokol units, the drop in Slet participation is not surprising. The fact that not all units that are listed as "active" (Appendix F) have gymnastics programs is a contributing factor to the decrease in participation. Thus, some units function primarily as social clubs. Never the less, there are several units that have very good facilities and viable gymnastics programs, e.g., New York, Greater Cleveland, Ennis, and Forth Worth. The reasons for the success of those units in maintaining or developing quality programs are noted in the next section of this chapter.

A New Generation and Environment

The Cultural Dilution

A new generation. Although some small towns and neighborhoods in some cities continue their Czech identity, not surprisingly, the passage of time has diminished memories and many of the traditions. Sokol still has many members with Czech backgrounds, but ethnic diversity is evident in the gym classes of virtually all units. These realities require an evaluation of the primary goals of Sokol, and a clear strategic plan to implement the goals. It is more difficult to maintain many of the Czech cultural activities, such as theater, costume balls, and language school, because Czech identity is far less common in the 21st century. Accordingly, very few youths of the current generation have the identity that seeks to foster this culture and the glorious history of the Sokol movement that helped create a nation for Czechs and Slovaks. This reality does not circumvent Sokol from being a major force in the training of youths.

Sokol's foundation. As clearly detailed by Miroslav Tyrš, Sokol's mission was the acquisition of physical, mental, and moral fitness, accomplished through a system of gymnastics training. Today, gymnastics is not the cornerstone of many Sokol units, but rather a single entity, if present. This reality requires that the mission of Sokol in the US must be reevaluated. The programs offered by various Sokol units differ, thus the original central focus is no longer obvious. An ethnic/cultural dilution, and consequently a loss of the historical perspective is certainly a key factor that has contributed to the loss of, in most cases, the historical Sokol gymnastics program. The environment of the current century has also played a major role in the demise, or reorientation of various Sokol units. There are, of course other factors that have blurred the primary objectives of the Sokol mission. These factors are addressed in the following sections.

Lack of Business Plans, and Well-trained Coaches and Instructors

The success of any gymnastics program that contributes to the fitness of various age groups requires leaders who understand the complexities of the skills required. In the past, some of the most successful units had full-time, paid, instructors, as well as assistants. The emphasis on using only volunteers by many Sokol clubs has limited their teaching of gymnastics. As costs have increased, the necessity of a good business plan has become more essential. Units that have been able to generate an income, i.e., by renting their facilities, sponsoring dances, or other business avenues, were more likely to maintain their programs. Moreover, charging adequate fees for their gymnastics classes has enabled units to hire well-trained instructors, and consequently develop or maintain strong programs, e.g., Fort Worth, Cleveland, and New York.

De-emphasis of Gymnastics

At the heart of Sokol's identity is, as noted above, the system of gymnastics, which in many instances, is only one of several options today, an indication that the Sokol idea, as originally developed, is no longer the core mission of most Sokol clubs. Although Sokol has traditionally included other fitness and sport opportunities, they were not of equivalents of gymnastics. In reviewing Sokol Olomouc's problems in 1879, Tyrš noted that one core problem was their lack of an adequate gymnastic program. This current de-emphasis of gymnastics is evident from many observations. One especially noteworthy fact is that recent gymnastic Slets did not offer high level divisions in their gymnastic competitions. Thus, gymnasts who qualified for advanced levels were not encouraged to participate. Traditional Sokol competitions offered four levels (divisions): low, intermediate, high, and championship. The de-emphasis of gymnastics that occurred is not surprising when there is a lack of trained staff, availability of adequate class days and time, and a business plan to facilitate the programs. The proliferation of private gymnastic clubs in the 1980s was a clear signal that gymnastics training was valued by many families. As Riha (1989, 10) noted, parental involvement in the children's classes is characteristic of these clubs. Their system of training is based on a program of skill levels formulated by the United States Gymnastics Federation (now USA Gymnastics). Most Sokol Units failed to grasp the opportunity of becoming a magnet for children interested in learning gymnastic skills, and, for some, competing in the sport. As demonstrated by the private gymnastic clubs, the best candidates for learning gymnastics skills are young children, i.e., tots and pre-juniors. In many cases, Sokol units did not encourage these age groups to learn adequate gymnastics skills. Under such a circumstance, youngsters may choose another activity or a private gymnastics club.

A Broader Menu of Activities

The idea of a broader menu of activities, such as the traditional YMCA program, could still provide benefits to youths and adults, but to do so would require an expansion of the hours that the facilities are open, and providing additional instructors. This option is not feasible for most units. Only a few with an adequate staff, facilities and a good business plan can offer several sport and fitness options. Sokol, like the Turners, provided a program that was limited or lacking elsewhere. For that reason, they were instrumental in introducing gymnastics to high schools, as noted in Chapter 5. High school programs appeared to peak between 1960 and 1980, but then diminished because of costs. It was after these decades that the proliferation of gymnastic clubs occurred throughout the US. These clubs survived because they offered well-trained instructors and training sessions on multiple days of the week. This was possible only because the students paid fees that covered the costs of instruction and facilities. One major problem with these programs is that many families can not afford the costs of the training. However, Sokol units were in a better position of offer gymnastics programs at costs lower than those offered by the many private clubs. First, Sokols are non-profit clubs. Second, adult members could have been encouraged to help with the costs of the programs via donations and fund-raising. Thus, high quality gymnastics programs could have been made available at costs that many families may have been able to afford.

Limited Access to Facilities and Limited Programs

Another challenge for many Sokols has been an inadequate number of hours for their gymnastic classes for a given group. Most often a class meets only once per week, and access to the gymnasium at other times is not available. These limitations circumvent both learning skills and the development of physical fitness. Yet this type of schedule is the rule, rather than the exception in most Sokol gyms. In reviewing the class schedules of various units, one finds that not all week days have classes scheduled, a fact that indicates an under utilization of facilities and instruction.

Sokol's Future

Community service and the training of youth should be key objectives of any fitness organization. Instilling the virtues of discipline, sportsmanship, and democracy should not be limited to a historical Sokol only, they should be foundations for any organization that is in a position to influence the development of youth. Therefore, each club needs to define its purpose, goals, and limitations in order to have an impact on the youth of America. There are many youngsters who are missing the opportunities that Sokol can provide. As an important historical cornerstone, the concepts and spirit of the Tyrš' philosophy can still be included if a Sokol club has an educational mission. The focus of the Sokol mission should be on youth, especially tots, because they are most impressionable and learn skills more enthusiastically than most teens and adults. No doubt some Sokol units, if fully committed, can provide meaningful programs, as evidence by those that serve as role models.

Tots gymnastic class at Sokol Cedar Rapids, Iowa.

Newer facilities in two very active Sokols: Karel Havlíček Borovsky, Ennis, Texas (top), and Greater Cleveland (bottom).

Table 1

Growth of Czech Sokol during its first fifty years (data are based on report from Cervenka, 1920)

Year	Number of Clubs	Number of Members	% Change
1865	19	1,712	
1871	114	10,516	(+514)
1875	72	7,191	(-32) *
1883	105	11,197	(+56)
1888	171	19,817	(+76)
1897	466	43,870	(+121)
1902	671	52,169	(+19)
1910	916	95,077	(+82) **
1912	1,091	119,183	(+25)

* Decline in number of clubs and members was ascribed to political dissention, lack of an adequate gymnastics program in some clubs, and financial mismanagement.

** Women were included in membership for first time, and were 14,585 of the total.

Table 2

Czech Sokol Slet Participants (1882–1948)

Slet	Year	Men	Women	Juniors and Children	Spectators
I	1882	720			3,420
II	1891	2,473			7,000
III	1895	5,000 +			30,000 +
IV	1901	6,705	867	1,600	50,000 +
V	1907	7,600	2,500	2,800	100,000 +
VI	1912	18,000	5,600	8,057	120,000 +
VII	1920	23,839	15,000	13,200	500,000 * +
VIII	1926	29,800	14,100	52,963	825,000 * +
IX	1932	35,016	25,000	60,325	1 million * +
X	1938	28,600	26,648	94,772	2 million * +
XI	1948	150,000	(men & women)	250,000	2 million * +

Data are from *ČOS* (Czech Sokol Organization) and American Sokol Organization.
* Several days attendance in the stadium.
+ Actual number exceeds that of estimate.

Table 3

Earliest Czech-American Sokol Clubs (Units)

1865	St. Louis
1866	Gymnastic Unit Sokol (Chicago)
1867	New York; Svornost (Morriania, NY)
1868	Milwaukee; Slovanska Lipa (Chicago); Czech-American (Chicago)
1870	Perun/Cleveland
1872	Blesk (Baltimore)
1873	Tyrs-Cedar Rapids
1875	Budivoj (Detroit)
1876	Fuegner (Long Island, NY); Czech-American (Manitowoc, WI)
1877	Omaha; Cechie (Chicago)
1878	Czech-American (Kewaunee, WI)
1879	Pilsen (Chicago); Cech (Cleveland)
1880	Wilber, NE
1881	Czech-American (Braidwood, IL)
1882	St. Paul
1883	Westfield, MA
1884	Crete, NE
1886	Fuegner Sultan (Long Island)
1887	Prague, NE
1888	South Omaha; California (Chicago); Praha (Chicago)
1889	Podlipny (Detroit); Mladočech (Racine, WI)
1890	Slávský (Cicero, IL); Tabor (Chicago); Klatovsky (Chicago); Zizka (Bruno, NE)
1891	Plattsmouth, NE
1892	Chicago; Nova Vlast (Cleveland); Karel Stulik (Schuyler, NE); Hornik (Coal City, IL)

Table 4

National Union Slets

Slet	Year	Site	Number of Competitors	Total Number of Participants *
I	1879	New York	19M (7 units)	
II	1881	Detroit	39M (13 units)	
III	1884	Chicago	47M (12 units)	
IV	1887	New York	41M (12 units)	
V	1891	Milwaukee	123M	
VI	1893	Chicago	194M (24 units)	360M, 275W, 368J
VII	1900	Cleveland	119M	225M, 115W, 240J, 135C
VIII	1904	St. Louis	197M, 66W	700 total
IX	1909	Chicago	274M, W?	302M, 300W, 800J+C
X	1914	Omaha	200M,150W	200M, 150W, 200J, 175C

Data are from Barcal, 1990, and American Sokol Organization.

M, Men; W, Women; J, Juniors; C, Children.

* Competitors and non-competitors in mass calisthenic displays and special numbers.

Table 5

American Sokol Organization Slets (1921–2017)

Slet	Year	Site	Number of Competitors	Total Number of Participants *
I	1921	Chicago	258M, 208W	367M, 369W, 229J, 391C
II	1925	Chicago	617M, 320W	1,382MW, 434J, 491C
III	1929	Chicago	331M, 288W, 115J	1,092MW, 483J, 623C
IV	1933	Chicago	197M, 214W, 202J	3,403
V	1937	Chicago	219M, 203W, 369J	2,900
VI	1941	Chicago	440M, 626W, 436J	4,000 +
VII	1947	Chicago	281M, 309W, 376J	1,828
VIII	1953	Chicago	247M, 371W, 289J	1,270
IX	1957	Berwyn	597MW, 470J	1,528
X	1961	Berwyn	290M, 372W, 622J	2,253
XI	1965	Berwyn	231M, 390W, 700J	2,340
XII	1969	Berwyn	52M, 84W, 497J	1,748
XIII	1973	Berwyn	61M, 112W, 650J	1,358
XIV	1977	Berwyn	867MWJ + 68 Rhythmics #	1,592
XV	1981	Ft. Worth	684MWJ + 10 Rhythmics	1,328
XVI	1985	Berwyn	589MWJ + 32 Rhythmics	1,600
XVII	1989	Omaha	402MWJ + 29 Rhythmics	1,190
XVIII	1993	Berwyn	581MWJ + 71 Rhythmics	1,469
XIX	1997	Berwyn	497MWJ + 46 Rhythmics	1,404
XX	2001	Detroit	350MWJ + 33 Rhythmics	604
XXI	2005	Berwyn	360MWJ + 45 Rhythmics	950
XXII	2009	Ft. Worth	320MWJ + 16 Rhythmics	750
XXIII	2013	Milwaukee	221MWJ + 16 Rhythmics	668
XXIV	2017	Cedar Rapids	231MWJ	620

Data are from Barcal, 1990, and American Sokol Organization, and Mike Dropka, 2019 (personal communication).

* Competitors and non-competitors in mass calisthenic displays and special numbers.

M, Men; W, Women; J, Juniors; C, Children.

#, Rhythmic Gymnastics competitions were introduced in 1977; the number of competitors is indicated for the next nine Slets.

Appendix A
First National Unity Sokol: Units and Districts (1894)

Eastern District (New York City)

New York	Newark
Fuegner (Long Island City)	Westfield (MA)
Blesk (Baltimore)	Svornost (Morrisania, NY)

Western District (Omaha)

Zika (Bruno, NE)	Schuyler (NE)
Crete (NE)	So. Omaha
Linwood (NE)	St. Louis
Omaha	Wilber (NE)
Cesky Lev (Oxford Junction, IA)	Cedar Rapids (IA)
Plattsmouth (NE)	

Central District (Milwaukee)

Cech (Cleveland)	Podlipny (Detroit)
Cech American (Manitowoc, WI)	East (Saginaw, MI)
Nova Vlast (Cleveland)	Milwaukee
Budivoj (Detroit)	Mladočech (Racine, WI)

Chicago District (Chicago)

Cech American (Braidwood, IL)	Cechie (Chicago)
Klatovsky (Chicago)	Tabor (Chicago)
Plzensky (Chicago)	Tyrš (Chicago)
Chicago	Horwick (Coal City, IL)
Slovanska Lipa (Chicago)	Praha, Town of Lake (Chicago)

Data from Barcal, 1991

Appendix B
Sokol Union in America
Units and Districts (1917)
Eastern District (New York City)

* Blesk (Baltimore)	East Islip (Long Island)	Bridgeport (OH)
* Havlíček (Cleveland)	Svornost (Bronx, NY)	Fuegner-Tyrš (Dayton, OH)
* Nova Vlast (Cleveland)	Schenectady (NY)	Detroit
Cleveland	Rip (Pittsburg)	Nova Vlast (Transverse City, MA)
Cech (Cleveland)	*Little Ferry (NJ)	Masaryk (Flint, MI)
Tyrš (Cleveland)	Westfield (MA)	
* New York	Philadelphia	
* Fuegner, Long Island City	Irvin (PA)	
Newark	Lorain (OH)	
*Bohemia (Long Island)	Moravian (Toledo)	

Central District (Chicago)

Pilsen (Chicago)	* Slavoj (Chicago)	Berwyn (IL)
* Chicago (Chicago)	* Fuegner (Chicago)	Karel Jonas (Cicero, IL)
* Tabor (Chicago)	* Vysehrad (Chicago)	Slovan (Lyons, IL)
* Rozvoj (Chicago)	Chechie (Chicago)	* Mladočech (Racine, WI)
* Slávský (Chicago)	Oak Park (IL)	Melnik (Maribel, WI)
* Havlíček-Tyrš (Chicago)	Milwaukee	*Klomensky

Western District (Omaha)

* Omaha	* Howells (NE)	* St. Louis
* Fuegner-Tyrš (So. Omaha)	* Ord (NE)	* Cech-American (Manitowoc, WI)
* Schuylef (NE)	* Ravenna (NE)	* Edwardsville (IL)
* Crete (NE)	* Komensky (Brainard, NE)	* St. Paul
* Tyrš & Tyršova (Cedar Rapids, IA)	* Hvezda Zapadu (Black Wolf, KS)	* Owatonna (MN)
* Iowa City	Karel Jones (Wilson, KS)	* Minneapolis
* Plattsmouth (NE)	Timken (KS)	* Hopkins (MN)
Jiri Podebrad (Clarkson, NE)	Oklahoma City	* Montgomery (MN)
* Jonas (Abie, NE)	* Praha (Prague, OK)	* New Prague (MN)
* Dodge (NE)	* Vysehrad (Lucas, KS)	

Appendix B
Continued

Southern District (Dallas)

* Zizka/Libuse (Dallas)	Ft. Worth	Granger (TX)
Karel Havlíček Borovksy (Ennis)	Galveston	Jan A. Komensky (Guy, TX)

Pacific District (San Francisco)

* San Francisco	* Malin (OR)	Scio (OR)
* Los Angeles	Oakland	Portland

Data are from Barcal, 1991.

* Separate men's and women's units

Appendix C
American Sokol Organization
Units and Districts (1933)

Eastern District

Curtis Bay, MD	* Little Ferry, NJ	* Schenectady, NY
* Blesk, Baltimore	* Newark	Westfield, MA
Fuegner, Long Island, NY	* Philadelphia	Petersburg, VA
* New York		

Northeastern District

Cleveland	* Detroit	Fuegner, Azalia, MI
Cech-Havlíček, Cleveland	Moravan, Toledo	Owosso, MI
Nova Vlast, Cleveland	Rip, Pittsburg	Banister, MI
Tyrš, Cleveland		

Central District

* Chicago	Fuegner, Chicago	East St. Louis, IL
Cechie, Chicago	* Berwyn, IL	Edwardsville, IL
* Tabor, Berwyn, IL	* Rozvoj, Irving Park, IL	Stickney, IL
Czech-American, Chicago	* Cedar Rapids	Manitowoc, WI
* Slávský, Cicero, IL	* Milwaukee	Polivkas Corner, WI
* Havlíček-Tyrš, Chicago	* Mladočech, Racine, WI	Menominee, MI
*Tabor, Berwyn	Slovanska Lipa, St. Louis	

Western District

* Omaha	Winner, SD	Ord, NE
Sokolice Tyrš, Omaha	* Crete, NE	Burwell, NE
* South Omaha	Dodge, NE	Niobrara, NE
Wilber, NE	Schuyler, NE	Milligan, NE
Clarkson, NE	Abie, NE	Wagner, SD
Tyndall, SD	Prague, NE	Cuba, KN
Verdegre, NE		

Appendix C
Continued

Northern District

St. Paul	New Prague, MN	Lankin, ND
Minneapolis	Meadowlands, MN	Cadott, WI
Hopkins, MN	Pine City, MN	Haugen, WI
Owatonna, MN	Mandan, ND	Phillips, WI

Southwestern District

Praha, OK	Karel Havlíček, Yukon, OK	Vysehrad, Lucas, KS
Oklahoma City	Caldwell, KS	Karel Jonas, Wilson, KS

Southern District

Zizka, Dallas	Komensky, Guy, TX	Floresville, TX
Fort Worth	Galveston	Corpus Christi, TX
Karel Havlíček, Ennis, TX	Rowena, TX	San Antonio
Taylor, TX	Placedo, TX	

Pacific District

* Los Angeles	Malin, OR	Portland
Oakland	Scio, OR	Seattle
San Francisco		

Data from *American Sokol, Vol. 55 No. 7,* 1933.

* Separate men's and women's units

Appendix D
American Sokol Organization: Units and Districts (1961)

Eastern District (New York City)

* Blesk (Baltimore)	Philadelphia	* Newark
Curtis Bay (MD)	Belcamp (MD)	Washington (DC)
Little Ferry (NJ)	Fuegner (Long Island)	* Schenectady
New York		

Northeastern District (Cleveland)

Cleveland-Chech-Havlíček	Rip (Pittsburgh)	Tyrš (Cleveland)
Nova Vlast (Cleveland)	* Detroit	Moravian (Toledo)

Central District (Chicago)

Americky (Chicago)	Rozvoj (Chicago)	* Tabor (Berwyn)
Berwyn	Cechie (Chicago)	* Town of Lake (Chicago)
Brookfield	Fuegner (So. Chicago)	West Suburban
* Chicago	* Havlíček-Tyrš (Chicago)	* Milwaukee
St. Louis	Slávský (Cicero)	* Mladočech (Racine, WI)
Pilsen (Chicago)		

Western District (Omaha)

* Cedar Rapids	* Omaha	Wilber
* Crete	* South Omaha	Schuyler

Northern District (St. Paul)

St. Paul	Pine City (MN)	Hopkins (MN)
Minneapolis		

Southern District (Dallas)

Ft. Worth	Houston	Praha (Prague OK)
Corpus Christi	Karel Havlíček Borovsky (Ennis)	Karel Havlíček (Yukon, OK)
Zizka (Dallas)		

Pacific District (San Francisco)

* San Francisco	* Fresno	Portland
* Los Angeles	Seattle	Scio (OR)

Data from American Sokol Organization.

* Separate men's and women's units

106—

Appendix E
American Sokol Organization: Units and Districts (1994)

Eastern District (New York City)

New York	Schenectady (NY)	Washington (DC)
Fuegner (Long Island)	Belcamp (MD)	Miami
* Little Ferry (NJ)	Curtis Bay (MD)	Baltimore

Northeastern District (Cleveland)

Greater Cleveland	Detroit	

Central District (Chicago)

Berwyn	Chicagoland	Slávský (Cicero)
Brookfield	* Tabor (Berwyn)	Stickney (IL)
Cechie (Chicago)	Naperville	St. Louis
Havlíček-Tyrš (Chicago)	* Milwaukee	Racine (WI)
Ceska Sin (Chicago)	Town of Lake (Chicago)	

Western District (Omaha)

Omaha	Minnesota	Crete
Cedar Rapids	* So. Omaha	Wilber

Southern District (Dallas)

Zizka (Dallas)	West	Taylor (TX)
Ft. Worth	Corpus Christie	Karel Havlíček (Yukon, OK)
Karel Havlíček Borovsky (Ennis)	Houston	

Pacific District (San Francisco)

San Francisco	Los Angeles	Fresno

Data from American Sokol Organization.

* Separate men's and women's units

Appendix F
American Sokol Organization: Units and Districts (2008)

Eastern District (New York City)

New York	Washington (DC)	Curtis Bay (MD)
Little Ferry (NJ)	Baltimore	Philadelphia

Northeastern District (Cleveland)

Greater Cleveland	Detroit	

Central District (Chicago)

Chicagoland	Stickney (IL)	Ceska Sin (Cleveland)
Naperville (IL)	* Tabor (Berwyn, IL)	Town of Lake (Chicago)
Sprit (Brookfield, IL)	St. Louis	Milwaukee

Western District (Omaha)

Omaha	Cedar Rapids	Wilber (NE)
South Omaha	* Crete (NE)	Minnesota

Southern District (Ennis)

Corpus Christi	K. Havlíček Borovsky (Ennis)	West (TX)
Fort Worth	K. Havlíček (Yukon, OK)	Zizka (Dallas)
Houston		

Pacific District (San Francisco)

San Francisco	Los Angeles	Fresno

Data from Sokol American Organization

* Separate men's and women's units

References Cited

Agnew HL. *The Czechs and the Lands of the Bohemian Crown.* Hoover Institute Press, Stanford University, Stanford, California 2004.

Bábela M, Oborný J. Dr. Miroslav Tyrš—Father of the Sokol and Philosophy of the Sokol. *Science of Gymnastics Journal* 10:313–329, 2018.

Balch EG. *Our Slavic Fellow Citizens.* Charities Publishing, New York 1910.

Barcal S. *History of the American Sokol Organization 125 years 1865–1990.* Unpublished manuscript, American Sokol Organization, Chicago 1991.

Bažant J. *Nation and Art. From Miroslav Tyrš* and *Max Dvořák,* and back. ARS 44:15–25, 2011.

Bednar C. *The Sokols and Their Endeavor.* Publ. Educational and Publicity Committee of the Slovak Gymnastic Union Sokol in the United States 1948.

Bicha KD. The Czechs in Wisconsin History. *Wisconsin Magazine of History* 53:194–203, 1970.

Biroczi D. *Czechs in America: The Maintenance of Czech Identity in Contemporary America.* Thesis. University West Bohemia, Pilsen 2003.

Brodin H. *Per Henrik Ling and His Impact on Gymnastics (in Swedish).* Sven Med Tidskr 12: 61–68, 2008.

Bubeníček R. *A History of Czechs in Chicago.* K. Chott, translator. Czech and Slovak American Geneology Sociey of Illinois, Chicago 2011.

Burian M. *Sokolský Odpor.* Česka Obec Sokolská, Prague 2005.

Butterworth H. *The Horizontal Bar.* Copyright by Horace Butterworth 1902.

Čapek T. *The Čech (Bohemian) Community of New York.* Czechoslovak Section of America's Making, Inc. New York 1921.

Čapek T. *American Czechs in Public Office.* Czech Historical Society of Nebraska, Omaha 1940.

Čapek T. *Naše Amerika (Our America),* Národní rada Ceskoslovenská, Prague 1926.

Čapek T. *Moje Amerika: Vzpomínkya Úvahy, 1861–1934 (My America: Reminiscences and Reflections, 1861–1934).* F. Boravy, Prague 1935.

Čapek T. *The Cechs (Bohemians) in America: A Study of their National, Cultural, Political, Social, Economic and Religious Life.* Houghton Mifflin Co., Boston and New York 1920.

Cather W. *My Antonia.* Houghton Mifflin, Boston 1918.

Cermak J. *Dr. Miroslav Tyrš. Founder of the Gymnastics Organization Sokol.* American Sokol Educational and Physical Cultural Organization, Chicago 1966.

Cervenka V. U. *Kolébky Sokola.* Prague 1920

Chada J. *The Czechs in the United States.* SVU Press, Washington, DC 1981.

Chroust DZ. *Bohemian Voice: Contention, Brotherhood and Journalism Among Czech People in America 1860–1910.* PhD Dissertation. Texas A&M University 2000.

Cumiskey FJ. A History of Gymnastics. The Olympiads and the Intervening Years. *International Gymnastics* 1983.

Czechoslovak Legions 1914–1918 and the Association of Czechoslovak Legionnaires (M. Mojžíš, ed.) 2017.

Dimond M. The Sokol and Czech Nationalism 1918–1948. *Proc. British Academy 140: 185–205, 2007.*

Dubovický I. *Češi v Americe (Czechs in America).* Translation: Linda Paukertová, Prague edition 2003

Dusek PP Jr. Marie Pravaznik: Her life and Contributions to Physical Education. Ph.D. Thesis, University of Utah 1981.

Dvornik F. *Czech Contributions to the Growth of the United States.* Benedictine Abbey Press, Chicago 1961.

Fornůskova J. *Factors that drove Czecho-Slovaks to Emigrate to the US.* Bachelor Thesis, Thomas Bata Univ., Zlin, Czech Republic 2009.

Frederick AB. Gymnastics: Then and Now and What Next? Balance beam. *Int Gymnastics Magazine* 26:55–57, 1984.

Gajdoš A, Provaznikova M, Banjak SJ. 150 years of the Sokol Gymnastics in Czechoslovakia, Czech and Slovak Republic. *Science of Gymnastics Journal* 4:5–26, 2012

Garver BM. *The Young Czech Party 1874–1901 and the Emergence of the Multiparty System.* Yale University Press, New Haven 1978.

Goodbody J. *The Illustrated History of Gymnastics.* Stanley Paul and Company, London 1982.

Grossfeld A. A History of United States Artistic Gymnastics. *Science of Gymnastics Journal* 2:5–28, 2010.

Grossfeld A. Changes During the 110 Years of the World Artistic Championships. *Science of Gymnastics Journal* 6:5–27, 2014.

Guth J. *Hry Olympické za starověku a za dod nejnovějsich,* Prague 1896.

Habenicht J. *Dějíny Čechův Amerických (History of the American Czechs).* Hlas, St. Louis 1910.

Hanzlik J. *Začiaty Českej A Slovenskej Emigracie do USA; (The Beginning of Czech and Slovak Emigration to the USA.)* Zbornik statí Bratislava Vydavatelstvo Slovenskej Akademie Ved, 1970.

Havlíček V. *The Czechoslovak Sokol Prague: Information Department of the Executive Committee of the XI Sokol Congress (Slet),* Prague 1948.

Havlíček V. *The Sokol Festival.* SFINX LTD Publishers, Prague 1948.

Horak J. *Assimilation of Czechs in Chicago. A sociological analysis of the process of assimilation in the Czech community in Chicago.* PhD dissertation, University of Chicago, Chicago 1920.

Jandasek L. The Sokol Movement in Czechoslovakia. *Slavonic and East European Review* 11: 65–80, 1932.

Jandásek L. *Sokol-občan.* Prague 1934.

Jandásek L, Pelikan J. *Stručné dějiny Sokolstva 1862–1912 (2nd Ed),* New York 1952.

Jaros RE. *Sokol Gathering in the New World.* KNA Press Inc, Kennett Square, Pennsylvania 1992

Jelinek J, Zmrhal J. Sokol Educational and Physical Culture Association. American Sokol Union, Chicago 1944.

Jerabek E. *Czechs and Slovaks in North America: A Bibliography.* SVU Press, Washington, DC 1976.

Jožák J. K Historie Českého Sokola v USA (1865–1914). *In Sborník Státniho Ú Středního Archivu v Praze,* Prague 1998.

Kabes OM. Women in the Sokol Movement. Paper read at Czechoslovak Society of Arts and Sciences North American Conference, Cedar Rapids, Iowa; June 26–28, 2003.

Kann RA. *The Multinational Empire: Nationalism and National Reform in the Habsburg Monarchy 1848–1918,* Vol 2, Empire Reform. Columbia University Press, New York 1950.

Kolár F, Kössl J. Origin and development of the Czech and Czechoslovak Olympic Committee. *Journal Olympic History 2:11–26,* 1994.

Komanická M. *Dějny Sokola Praha Vršovice 1870–1938.* Diploma Thesis, Charles University, Prague 2010.

Korbel J. *Twentieth-Century Czechoslovakia.* Columbia University Press, New York 1977.

Kovtun G. *The Czechs in America.* The Library of Congress European Reading Room. Area studies, European Division 2009.

Kral, EA. The community reborn through celebration of its heritage. *Slovo* 18: NCSML Summer 3:24–27, 2002.

Krejčí J. *Czechoslovakia at the Crossroads of European History.* Ibtauris & Co. Ltd Pub., London and New York 1990.

Laska V. *The Czechs in America 1633–1977. A Chronology of Fact & Book.* Oceana Publ. Inc., Dobbs Ferry, New York 1978.

Ledbetter E. *The Czechs of Cleveland.* Cleveland Americanization Committee. Mayor's Advisory War Committee. Cleveland 1919.

Lejková-Koeppl M. "The Sokol Movement"—A Tribute to the National Revival and Culture of the Czechoslovak Nation, in *The Czechoslovakia Past and Present.* Vol. II, M. Rechcigl Jr. Mouton, Paris 1968

Loken NC, Willoughby RJ. *Complete Book of Gymnastics (2nd Ed)* Prentice-Hall, Inc. Englewood Cliffs, New Jersey 1967.

Macháček F. The Sokol Movement: Its Contribution to Gymnastics. *Slavonic Review* 1938; 17:73.

Machann C, Mendl JW. Movement and Growth, Chapter 2 in *Krásna Amerika: A Study of the Czechs in Texas 1831–1939;* Eakin Press, Austin 1983.

McNamara KJ. *Dreams of a Great and Small Nation.* Public Affairs, New York 2016.

Mareš F. *Nebraska, Kansas Czech Settlers 1891–1895.* Compiled by Margie Sobotka. Unigraphic, Evansville, Indiana 1980.

Miller KD. *The Czecho-Slovaks in America.* George H Doran, New York 1922.

Nešpor ZR. Religious Processes in Contemporary Czech Society. *Czech Sociological Review* 40: 282–284, 2004.

Nolte CE. "Every Czech a Sokol!": Feminism and Nationalism in the Czech Sokol Movement. *Austrian History Yearbook* 24:79–100, 1993.

Nolte CE. *The Sokol in the Czech Lands to 1914. Training for the Nation.* Palgrave MacMillan, Great Britain 2002

Nolte CE. Our Brothers Across the Ocean: The Czech Sokol in America to 1914. *In Gymnastics, A Transatlantic Movement from Europe to America.* (G. Pfister, editor) Routledge Taylor and Francis Group, London and New York 2011.

Nolte CE. "All for One! One for All!" *The Federation of Slavic Sokols and the Failure of Neo-Slavism in Constructing Nationalities in East Europe.* PM Judson and ML Rozenblit, editors, Berghahn Books, New York 2005.

Pánek J, Tůma O, et al. *A History of the Czech Lands.* Charles University, Prague 2009.

Památník Sokola Pražského. Printed by J. Otty, Prague 1883

Památník T.J. Sokol v New Yorku. 1867–1917. New York Printing, New York 1917

Pienkos DE. One Hundred Years Young: A History of the Polish Falcons of America 1887–1987. *East European Monographs,* Boulder, Colorado 1987.

Prchal KM. *Educational Directors!* Unpublished document, American Sokol Organization, Chicago 1949.

Pravaznikova M. *To Byl Sokol,* KE Macana, Praha 1991.

Rechcigl J. *Czech Americans Timeline. Chronology of Milestones in History of Czechs in America.* Authorhouse LLC, Bloomington, Indiana 2013.

Riha J. Sokol—the Future is Yours. In *Program Book, XVII American Sokol Slet, 1989,* Omaha.

Sayer D. *The Coasts of Bohemia: A Czech History.* Princeton University Press, Princeton, New Jersey 1998.

Schmidt AB. Rhythmic Gymnastics. New Olympic Sport. *J Physical Ed Rec Dance* 55: 70–71, 1984.

Sinkmager J. Bohemians of the United States. *Catholic Encyclopedia Vol. 2,* 1913.

Smith R. Saving pilsen's 100-year-old Sokols, the historic athletic clubs. *Curbed Chicago Newsletters* June 14, 2019

Souvenir Book XII. Slet of the American Sokol Slet in Chicagoland, Published by American Sokol Organization, June 25–29, 1969.

Stavařová I. *The Czech Americans.* Thesis, Masaryk University, Brno 2009.

Svoboda, JG. Czech-Americans: The Love of Liberty. *Nebraska History* 1993; 74: 109–119.

Tanzone DF. An overview of our 90 years of fraternal service. *Slovak Catholic Falcon* 1995.

Tanzone, DF. Celebrating a Centennial of Faith Life and Witness. *The Slovak Catholic Federation* 2005.

Tyrš M. (Translated by J Cihak). *Our Task, Aim and Goal* (original in 1st Sokol periodical 1871). American Sokol Organization, Chicago 1948.

US Census Bureau 2007.

Vukašinovic V, Šiljak V, Křocič and Saša Vajíc. It Began with Gymnastics. *Physical Education and Sport Through the Centuries* 4:42–56, 2017.

Zizka E. *Czech Cultural Contributions.* Copyright by Ernest Zizka 1943.

Zwarg LF. Historical review of the development of apparatus exercises. *Int Gymnast* 23: TS-35–TS-37, 1981.

Made in the USA
Columbia, SC
06 July 2021

41460145R00067